PROBLEM SOLVING
WITH CODE

C# Programming through the Eyes of Faith

John D. Delano, Ph.D.

Scripture References Acknowledgment

Scripture quotations are from the ESV® Bible (The Holy Bible, English Standard Version®), Copyright © 2001 by Crossway, a publishing ministry of Good News Publishers. Used by permission. All rights reserved.

Printed in the United States of America.
First Edition: December 2024
ISBN - Paperback: 979-8-339-80655-4

For more information, contact:
John D. Delano
drjdelano@outlook.com
https://www.thedigitalpath.org

Cover designed by Getcovers

PREFACE

Welcome to *Problem Solving with Code*. This book is designed to take you on a journey through the fundamentals of programming while also challenging you to think critically and solve complex problems. Throughout the chapters, you'll explore concepts like object-oriented programming, decision structures, loops, arrays, lists, and inheritance, all while following along with Alex as he builds an adventure game that grows in complexity. At the heart of this journey is a biblical foundation that will encourage you to approach problem-solving with faith, purpose, and a deeper understanding of stewardship in your work.

Programming is about more than just writing lines of code. It's about understanding how to break down problems and craft effective solutions. My goal with this book is not only to teach you the technical skills you need but also to instill a mindset of perseverance and creativity when tackling challenges, both in coding and beyond.

To help you learn, all the code used in the book is available on GitHub. You can access the repository at *https://github.com/jdelano/ Problem-Solving-with-Code*, where you'll find the code used in this book, organized by chapter. Feel free to explore, experiment, and even modify the code as you progress through the book.

Happy coding!

Contents

"And God blessed them. And God said to them, 'Be fruitful and multiply and fill the earth and subdue it, and have dominion over the fish of the sea and over the birds of the heavens and over every living thing that moves on the earth.'"
Genesis 1:28 (ESV)

CHAPTER 1

INTRODUCTION TO PROBLEM SOLVING

Introduction

Welcome to your first step in learning to program with C#! This chapter will focus on one of the most fundamental skills you'll need as a programmer: problem-solving. Before you can write a single line of code, you need to know how to solve problems logically and efficiently.

Programming is essentially a tool we use to solve real-world problems through the power of computers. Whether it's building a game, managing business operations, or automating a task, everything starts with identifying a problem and coming up with a plan to solve it.

As Christian programmers, we can look to God's example as the ultimate problem-solver. In His infinite wisdom, God foresaw the consequences of man's fall into sin and, from the foundation of the world, provided the perfect solution through the redemptive work of Jesus Christ (Ephesians 1:4-7). God's plan of salvation was not a mere reaction but a deliberate, sovereign act to reconcile us to Himself. Made in the image of God (Genesis 1:27), we reflect His communicable attributes (those qualities of God that He shares with us), such as creativity, wisdom, and the ability to solve problems.

From the very beginning, God gave mankind the mandate to exercise dominion over creation (Genesis 1:28). God called us to exercise stewardship over His creation by bringing order, care, and purpose to the world. This stewardship includes not only our physical surroundings but also our talents, such as programming, as ways to serve others and honor Him. As Christian problem-solvers, our approach should be purposeful, thoughtful, and rooted in truth. We are called not only to fix immediate problems but to seek solutions that reflect God's character, marked by truth, integrity, and lasting impact.

Whether we are writing code, solving technical challenges, or addressing life's difficulties, we exercise a God-given capacity to bring order and purpose to the world. This reflects God's glory as we work to fulfill His mandate. Our problem-solving efforts, seen through the lens of stewardship, are an act of worship and a means to honor the Creator in all that we do.

The Problem-Solving Process

Below are five general steps to solving programming problems, but they can also be applied generally to many areas of life. We'll use these five steps throughout this book.

- **Understand the Problem**: Read and analyze the problem carefully. Make sure you truly understand what is being asked before jumping to a solution.
- **Plan the Solution**: Break down the problem into smaller parts, then outline the steps required to solve it.
- **Implement the Solution**: Write the code using a programming language (in our case, C#).
- **Test the Solution**: Run the program to see if it works. If it doesn't, figure out why and adjust.
- **Refine and Optimize**: Look for ways to make your solution more efficient or simpler.

Step 1. Understand the Problem

Let's look at a simple problem to see how this problem-solving process can be applied. Meet Alex Garcia, a passionate student with a love for programming and video games. He dreams of creating a fully immersive game world where players can explore, collect resources, and battle enemies. Alex is particularly excited about building a game where players feel a sense of accomplishment as they progress through different levels. However, to bring his vision to life, Alex must first solve some key programming challenges, starting with how to track and display the resources collected by players in the game. This problem will help him sharpen his problem-solving skills and get closer to creating his dream game.

To solve this problem, Alex begins with the first step of the problem-solving process described earlier, which is to understand the problem. What this means for Alex is that he needs to figure out exactly how many resources the player has collected at any given moment and display the total to the player. He needs to be certain that the number of resources is accurate and that the game keeps track of them consistently as the player progresses. This requires Alex to consider how the resource data is stored, updated, and ultimately shown to the player in a way that makes sense during game-play. Without a clear understanding of this foundation, it will be difficult for him to move forward and plan a solution that works well within his game world.

Step 2. Plan the Solution

Now that Alex understands the problem, the next step is to develop a plan for how to solve it. Much like in real life, where we often need to keep track of quantities and adjust them as needed (like tracking the amount of money saved or supplies gathered), Alex's game needs a system that can store and update the number of resources that players collect. To make this happen, Alex needs a way to store and update this information reliably as the player moves through the game world. This means creating a placeholder that can remember the value of the resources collected.

Introducing Variables

In programming, a **variable** is like a container that holds information for the program to use later. Alex needs to keep track of how many resources that his players have collected. This means Alex will use a variable to store the running total of the resources collected. As players collect more resources, the value of this variable will be updated.

You can think of a variable like a box that can hold a single value at a time. Alex can open the box and view or update the value inside whenever needed. For example, Alex might create a variable called `totalResources` and set it to `0` at the start of the game.

Pseudo-code

With an understanding of what the variable will do, Alex can now start planning his solution in more detail. Before diving into the actual code, it's often helpful to outline the steps of the program in plain language, creating a blueprint for the solution. This is where **pseudo-code** becomes a valuable tool. Pseudo-code is a way of describing what the program should do without worrying about the exact syntax of the programming language. For Alex, it's essential to have a clear picture of how the game will track resources and how each action will flow from one step to the next. By writing out pseudo-code, Alex can organize his thoughts and ensure that he doesn't miss any steps.

For example, Text Box 1.1 shows what the pseudo-code for Alex's game might look like. These simple steps break down the task into an easy-to-follow plan, ensuring that Alex captures each essential action. Moreover, pseudo-code can easily transition into actual code. Alex could type these steps as comments in his development environment, providing a natural outline for the code. He can then implement each step

---

Text Box 1.1: Pseudo-code

Create a variable `totalResources` and set it to `0`.
Prompt user for the number of resources collected.
Add the collected resources to `totalResources`.
Print out the `totalResources`.

---

underneath the corresponding comment, effectively turning the pseudo-code into fully functional code.

Activity Diagrams

In addition to pseudo-code, another helpful tool for planning a solution is an **activity diagram**. While pseudo-code is perfect for outlining steps in plain language, an activity diagram provides a visual representation of the program's flow, showing how each action connects to the next in a structured format. This visual approach can be especially useful when planning more complex processes, where seeing the flow of actions helps clarify the logic of the program.

Alex can use the activity diagram shown in Figure 1.1 to represent the same steps outlined in his pseudo-code, offering a graphical perspective on the resource collection process. An activity diagram begins with an initial node, shown as a filled black circle, representing the start of the program flow. From this starting point, arrows guide the viewer through each action, showing the direction of the program's progression. Each

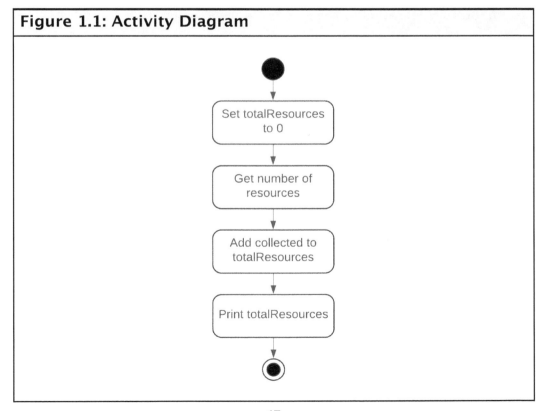

Figure 1.1: Activity Diagram

action is represented by an activity node, which is shown as a rectangle with rounded corners. The sequence then concludes at the terminal node, depicted as a circle with a smaller, black circle inside.

While pseudo-code is often sufficient for simpler problems, activity diagrams provide additional clarity for more complex scenarios. For many tasks, starting with pseudo-code can be a quick and efficient way to outline the steps, which can then be implemented directly as comments in the code. When visualizing the flow is essential, an activity diagram helps ensure that each action is accounted for, and that the logic flows correctly from one step to the next. By using both pseudo-code and activity diagrams where appropriate, Alex gains a deeper understanding of his program, providing a comprehensive blueprint for coding his solution.

Step 3. Implement the Solution

Now that Alex has a solid plan in place, it's time to turn this plan into a working program. At its core, a **program** is simply an ordered list of commands that tells the computer what to do, one step at a time. These commands are executed in a specific sequence, where the computer follows the instructions from top to bottom, one after the other. If the commands aren't in the right order, the program won't work as expected. In Alex's game, this means that each step needs to happen in a precise order for the game to track resources correctly.

Understanding Data Types

As Alex begins writing his code, the first step is to declare the variables he will use to store information, such as the total number of resources collected. In programming, declaring a variable means telling the computer what kind of information the variable will hold (its **data type**) and giving the variable a name so the program can reference it later. Importantly, we only specify the data type when the variable is declared. From that point on, we simply use the variable name to access or modify its value.

Variables come in different types depending on the kind of data they need to store. For example:

- `int`: This data type is used to store whole numbers, like 0, 5, or -10. In Alex's game, he will use `int` to store the number of resources collected, because resources will be counted as whole numbers.

- `string`: This type is used for text. If Alex wanted to store the player's name, we would use a `string` variable because player names may consist of letters, numbers, and symbols. Even though a string can contain numbers (such as a zip code), C# does not store those numbers as a numeric value but rather as a sequence of characters.

- `double`: This type is used to store decimal numbers, such as 3.14 or 9.99. While Alex's game doesn't need decimals yet, if he wanted to track the exact weight of the resources, for example, he could use a `double` to store that information.

- `char`: This type is used to store a single character, such as a letter, digit, or symbol. For example, if Alex wanted to represent a specific resource type with a single letter (like 'W' for wood or 'S' for steel), he could use a `char` variable. Unlike a string, which can hold multiple characters, `char` is limited to just one.

By selecting the correct data type, Alex ensures that the program knows what kind of information is being stored and can handle it correctly. Alex is now ready to turn his pseudo-code into C# code. Code Block 1.1 shows how Alex has attempted to implement his game world problem using variables and console input/output in C#. You'll notice a few things in the code that we haven't introduced yet, like `Console.Write()` and `Console.`

Code Block 1.1: Alex's Solution

```
 1  using System;
 2
 3  // Create a variable totalResources and set it to 0.
 4  int totalResources = 0;
 5
 6  // Prompt user for the number of resources collected.
 7  Console.Write("Enter number of resources collected: ");
 8  int collected = int.Parse(Console.ReadLine());
 9
10  // Add the collected resources to totalResources.
11  totalResources += collected;
12
13  // Print out the totalResources.
14  Console.WriteLine($"Total Resources: {totalResources}");
```

WriteLine() and how we take input from the user, but don't worry! We'll go through each line and explain exactly how everything works.

Let's take our time as we walk through this code, step by step. Each part is simple, but understanding how the parts fit together is important. As we go along, you'll see how these basic elements form the foundation of more complex programming ideas.

Line number 1 imports the System namespace, which gives us access to useful classes like Console that allow us to read from and write to the console. It's required to use features like Console.Write(), Console.WriteLine() or Console.ReadLine() in our program. Think of a namespace as a filing system where related classes and methods are grouped together for easy access. Later in the book, we'll explore and use other namespaces to use additional functionality in our programs. Using namespaces helps keep code organized, especially as our projects grow in complexity.

Line number 4 declares a variable called totalResources of type int to hold a whole number of resources. We set it equal to 0 because, at the start of the game, the player hasn't collected any resources yet. This variable will store the total number of resources as the player collects them.

In C#, anything following // is a comment. Comments like those in line numbers 3, 6, 10, and 13 are ignored by the compiler and do not affect the program's functionality. They are helpful for programmers to explain what specific parts of the code do, making the code easier to understand when you or someone else revisits it later.

In line number 7, the Console.Write() method prints a message to the console. In this case, it displays the text, Enter the number of resources collected:. This message is asking the user to input a number, which will be handled by the next line of code. Unlike Console.WriteLine(), the Console.Write() method does not move the cursor to a new line after displaying the message, so the cursor remains on the same line, waiting for the user to input a value immediately after the prompt. Another way to include a new line in the message is to use the newline character (\n). Similarly, the tab character (\t) can be used to insert horizontal space, which is useful for aligning text into columns or creating more visually organized output. For example, `Console.Write("Name\tScore\n")` would display a header with a tab between "Name" and "Score" and move to a new line for subsequent output.

Line number 8 captures the user's input. First, `Console.ReadLine()` reads the text entered by the user as a string (a sequence of characters), and then `int.Parse()` changes that input from a string to an integer, so we can perform arithmetic operations on it. The result is stored in a new integer variable named `collected`.

Line number 11 is where the player's collected resources are added to the total. The `+=` operator is shorthand for saying "add the value of the `collected` variable to the `totalResources` variable and store the result back in `totalResources`." Since the program starts with `totalResources` set to 0, this line simply updates `totalResources` with the number the user enters. Notice that when updating the variable, we don't need to include its data type (`int`), because the data type was already specified when the variable was declared. From this point onward, we simply refer to the variable by its name to update or retrieve its value.

Line number 14 uses **string interpolation** to display the total number of resources collected. In C#, string interpolation is done by placing a dollar sign ($) before the string and enclosing variables or expressions in curly braces ({}). Here, `$"Total Resources: {totalResources}"` embeds the current value of `totalResources` directly into the string. For example, if the player collected 10 resources, the console would display: `Total Resources: 10`.

Input and Output

In programming, input refers to the information we get from the user, while output is the information we display back to the user. These two components are essential for making programs interactive. Without input and output, a program would be unable to communicate or receive instructions from its user.

In Alex's game, for example, input comes from the player when they enter the number of resources they've collected. To capture that input, we use the `Console.ReadLine()` method. This method waits for the user to type something on the keyboard and press the Enter or Return key. However, it's important to note that `Console.ReadLine()` doesn't prompt the user with any text on its own. It simply pauses the program, waiting for input. If we want to give the user instructions on what to enter, we need to display a message first, using `Console.Write()`. This way, the player knows what to do. Code Block 1.2 shows how we might prompt the user for their name, wait for the user to provide an input, and then capture their response into a variable for later use.

Code Block 1.2: Console Input

```
1  Console.Write("Enter your name: ");
2  string name = Console.ReadLine();
```

Once we have the input, we can provide feedback to the user by displaying an output message. To do this, we use `Console.WriteLine()` again, which prints a message to the console. For example, let's say we want to greet the player, using the name they entered. Code Block 1.3 demonstrates how we can do this.

Code Block 1.3: Console Output

```
1  Console.WriteLine($"Hello, {name}");
```

In this line, `Console.WriteLine()` is used to print a message that includes the value of the name variable. Notice the syntax of the message includes the name variable inside of curly braces, relying on string interpolation that we saw earlier. In this case, {name} will be replaced by the current value of the name variable. If name is Alex, for example, the output will be: `Hello, Alex`.

String interpolation is a powerful feature because it allows us to construct messages dynamically, inserting the latest values of variables directly into the text we display. This makes it much easier to provide meaningful feedback to the user based on the program's current state.

Mathematical Operations

In programming, we often need to perform calculations. In Alex's game, for example, he used the += operator to add the collected resources to the player's total. But there are other mathematical operations that are just as important. Code Block 1.4 lists the basic mathematical operators in C#.

Code Block 1.4: Basic Mathematical Operators in C#

```
1  // Addition (+) adds two numbers together:
2  int result1 = 5 + 3; // result is 8
3
4  // Subtraction (-) subtracts one number from another:
5  int result2 = 5 - 3; // result is 2
6
7  // Multiplication (*) multiplies two numbers:
8  int result3 = 5 * 3; // result is 15
9
10 // Division (/) divides one number by another.
11 int result4 = 6 / 3; // result is 2
```

In Alex's game, we use the += operator to add the resources the player collects to the total. This is just shorthand for a longer operation like this: `totalResources = totalResources + collected;` The += operator saves us from repeating the variable name, making the code easier to write and understand. These operators allow us to manipulate numbers, making calculations a core part of how we manage game logic, track scores, or calculate totals.

Understanding the Semicolon

You may have noticed that each line of code in C# ends with a semicolon (;). This is important because, in C#, the semicolon is used to indicate the end of a complete statement. Think of it like a period in a sentence. Each time you finish giving the computer an instruction (like declaring a variable or printing something to the console), you use a semicolon to let the program know that this instruction is complete. Forgetting a semicolon will cause a syntax error, which means the code won't run properly until the error is fixed. As you write more code, using semicolons will become second nature, just like ending sentences with a period when you write.

Step 4. Test the Solution

Now that Alex has written his code, it's time for him to test it. Testing is a crucial step in programming because it helps ensure that the code behaves exactly how it should. For Alex, this means checking if his game correctly tracks the resources collected by players.

Alex runs his program, enters different numbers, and checks if the output matches what he expects. If something goes wrong or the result doesn't look right, he'll need to debug his code. Debugging involves finding and fixing mistakes, which might be small errors in logic, missing steps, or incorrect calculations. Text Box 1.2 shows an example test case that Alex might use.

Text Box 1.2: Example Test Case

User input: 20
Expected output: "Total resources collected: 20"

When Alex runs the program with this input, if the output matches his expectation, then the code is working as it should. But if he enters 20 and the program gives an unexpected output (e.g., 0 or a completely different number), Alex will need to check his logic. Did he forget to add the resources? Did he add the resources incorrectly? Is the input being processed correctly? Testing helps Alex identify these potential issues early on.

Step 5. Refine and Optimize

Now that Alex's code works, the next step is to optimize it. Even though the code is functioning, Alex knows there's often room for improvement. Optimization is all about making the code cleaner, more efficient, and easier to maintain in the future.

As Alex reviews his code, he looks for ways to simplify the logic. He asks himself if there are any unnecessary steps or operations he can remove. For example, he might consider whether his variable names clearly communicate their purpose or if the logic can be streamlined.

Alex also considers readability. While his code works, it should also be easy to understand for himself and others who might work on it later. He makes sure to use descriptive names for variables like `totalResources` and adds comments where necessary, explaining what each part of the code does. This will help anyone (including Alex) who revisits the code down the line to understand it quickly.

Finally, Alex thinks about future changes. His current program tracks resources for a single player, but what if he wants to track resources for multiple players in the future? Or add more complex features like different types of resources? By organizing his code in a way that can handle these potential changes, Alex can make sure the program is easy to modify later without having to rewrite everything.

In programming, optimization isn't just a one-time process. It's an ongoing mindset. As Alex becomes more experienced, he'll keep finding new ways to make his code both efficient and easy to work with.

Recap: Breaking Down Big Problems

In this chapter, Alex learned about the five-step process for solving problems, which forms the foundation of effective programming. The process involves understanding the problem thoroughly, planning a clear solution, implementing the plan by writing code, testing to ensure everything works as expected, and refining the solution to improve efficiency and readability. By following this structured approach, we can confidently tackle complex challenges step by step, ensuring thoughtful and reliable solutions. Let's put this foundational strategy in your problem-solving toolkit in Text Box 1.3.

Text Box 1.3: Problem–Solving Strategies

1. **Follow the Five-Step Problem-Solving Process**
   Understand the problem, plan the solution, implement the solution, test the solution, and finally refine and optimize it. This structured approach will help you systematically tackle any programming challenge you encounter.

Summary

In this chapter, we introduced the essential skills needed for effective problem-solving in programming. We learned about the five-step process for solving problems—Understanding the Problem, Planning the Solution, Writing the Code, Testing the Solution, and Refining and Optimizing— and how these steps can be applied to writing code.

We also introduced Alex Garcia, who is working on building his own game world. Through his problem of tracking player resources, we explored the use of variables to store and manipulate data in our programs. Additionally, we introduced the concept of pseudo-code, which helps organize our thoughts before writing actual code.

Finally, we saw how Alex turned his plan into a functional C# program and learned the importance of testing and optimizing code to ensure that it runs efficiently and produces the expected results.

With this foundational understanding of problem-solving and basic programming concepts, you're ready to continue your journey into more advanced topics, starting with object-oriented programming in the next chapter.

Review Questions

1. Why is problem-solving such an important skill for programmers to develop before writing any code? How does this relate to the concept of stewardship as outlined in the Bible?

2. What is the five-step process for solving programming problems introduced in this chapter? How can this process be applied to both coding and real-life problem-solving situations?

3. In the example of Alex's game, why is it important for him to fully understand the problem before jumping into writing code? What might happen if he skips this step?

4. How does the final step of problem-solving (optimization) relate to the idea of stewardship?

5. How does the concept of variables help Alex track the number of resources players collect in his game? What are other scenarios where variables could be useful in a program?

6. What is pseudo-code, and why is it helpful to write pseudo-code before starting to write actual C# code? How did Alex use pseudo-code to plan his solution for tracking resources?

7. In the C# code provided for Alex's game, why is it necessary to use the `Console.ReadLine()` and `int.Parse()` methods? What role do they play in gathering and processing user input?

8. Why is testing such an important part of the problem-solving process? What might Alex need to check for when testing his program to ensure it works correctly?

9. As a Christian programmer, how can your approach to solving problems reflect God's character and the biblical principle of bringing order and purpose to the world? How does this perspective influence the way you write and optimize code?

Practice Problems

1. **Tracking Savings**: Write a program that starts with a hard-coded initial value of $50 in savings. The program should then ask the user how much they added to their savings today. Finally, it should calculate and display the new total savings using string interpolation. Sample Output:

    ```
    Enter how much you added to your savings today: 20
    Total Savings: $70
    ```

2. **Mileage Tracker**: Write a program that starts with a hard-coded initial value of 100 miles driven (representing miles driven so far). The program should ask the user how many additional miles they drove today. The program will then display the new total miles driven. Sample Output:

    ```
    Enter the number of miles driven today: 50
    Total Miles Driven: 150
    ```

3. **Calculating Total Resources**: Write a program that asks the user how many units of wood and how many units of stone they have collected. The program should then calculate the total amount of resources and display it. Sample Output:

```
Enter the number of wood units collected: 20
Enter the number of stone units collected: 15
Total Resources Collected: 35
```

4. **Calories Burned**: Write a program that asks the user how many calories they burned while running and how many calories they burned while cycling. The program should then calculate and display the total calories burned. Sample Output:

```
Enter the calories burned while running: 300
Enter the calories burned while cycling: 200
Total Calories Burned: 500
```

5. **Remaining Funds**: Write a program that asks the user for their initial balance and the amount they spent. The program should subtract the spent amount from the initial balance and display the remaining funds. Sample Output:

```
Enter your initial balance: 500
Enter the amount spent: 200
Remaining Balance: 300
```

6. **Calculating Weekly Salary**: Write a program that asks the user for their hourly wage and the number of hours they worked this week. The program should calculate their total earnings for the week using multiplication and display the result. Sample Output:

```
Enter your hourly wage: 15
Enter the number of hours worked this week: 40
Total Weekly Earnings: $600
```

7. **Average Score**: Write a program that asks the user for the total score they earned across three levels of a game. The program should then calculate the average score by dividing the total score by 3 and display the result. Sample Output:

```
Enter the total score earned in three levels: 300
Average Score: 100
```

"Trust in the Lord with all your heart, and do not lean on your own understanding. In all your ways acknowledge him, and he will make straight your paths."
Proverbs 3:5-6 (ESV)

CHAPTER 2

INTRODUCTION TO OBJECT–ORIENTATION

Introduction

In the previous chapter, we learned about problem-solving and how to systematically work through challenges by following a structured process. Now, we'll build on that foundation by introducing object-oriented programming, an incredibly powerful way to organize your code and solve more complex problems.

As you start learning to program, it's important to think of your code as a way of modeling the real world. By thinking in terms of objects (real-world entities like players, scores, or resources), we can simplify large problems by breaking them down into smaller, more manageable parts. This is exactly what object-oriented programming allows us to do.

The idea of breaking down big problems into smaller, manageable parts aligns well with biblical principles of diligence, stewardship, and humility. Throughout Scripture, we are encouraged to approach challenges thoughtfully and with intentionality, trusting in God's wisdom rather than relying solely on our own understanding.

Proverbs often highlights the value of planning and wise decision-making. For example, Proverbs 21:5 (ESV) says, "The plans of the diligent lead to profit as surely as haste leads to poverty." This verse underscores the importance of carefully considering each step of a plan, rather than rushing through it. In the same way, when we face complex problems, we should be diligent in breaking them down into smaller tasks, ensuring that each part is thoughtfully considered and well-executed.

Breaking down problems into smaller parts also reflects the biblical concept of stewardship. In Luke 16:10 (ESV), Jesus says, "Whoever can be trusted with very little can also be trusted with much." This emphasizes the principle that handling smaller tasks well prepares us for larger ones. When we responsibly manage each part of a problem, we are practicing faithful stewardship. God calls us to be wise and diligent in the way we manage the tasks and responsibilities He places before us.

Breaking down a problem also reflects humility. Instead of trying to tackle everything at once, which can lead to frustration or burnout, breaking the problem down shows a recognition of our human limitations. We acknowledge that it's often better to work through smaller pieces and that we may need help along the way (whether from others or relying on God's strength). Proverbs 3:5-6 (ESV) reminds us to "Trust in the Lord with all your heart and lean not on your own understanding; in all your ways submit to Him, and He will make your paths straight." This principle of humility and dependence on God encourages us to approach challenges with patience and trust, seeking wisdom and guidance for each step. Whether we are programming or tackling everyday life challenges, God's Word encourages us to plan carefully, steward our resources well, and humbly trust in His guidance. Let's see how Alex can apply this strategy using the five-step problem-solving process.

Step 1. Understand the Problem

Alex is designing a game where players collect resources and earn points. The problem is that managing all these interactions as a single block of code would quickly become overwhelming. He needs a way to break down this complexity into smaller parts so that each player and resource can be managed independently.

When faced with a complex problem, it can feel overwhelming. However, breaking the problem down into smaller, more manageable pieces makes the solution clearer. One of the key problem-solving strategies we'll use throughout this book is to break down a large problem into its component parts. In programming, these "component parts" often correspond to classes and objects.

A **class** is like a blueprint that defines the attributes and behaviors of an object. For example, in Alex's game, a `Player` class might define characteristics like a player's name and score, as well as actions that the player can take, such as collecting resources. When Alex uses the `Player` class to create actual players in the game, these are called **objects**. Each player object will have its own unique data, like a specific name and score, while still following the overall structure defined by the `Player` class.

But how do we decide what responsibilities each class should handle? This is where the single responsibility principle comes into play. The **single responsibility principle** is a fundamental rule in object-oriented programming that encourages us to give each class one specific responsibility or role. By giving each class a focused responsibility, the code becomes easier to understand, develop, and maintain over time. For instance, in Alex's game world, a `Player` class handles everything related to a player's actions and information, while a `Resource` class is responsible for managing the amount and type of a specific resource. Each class has a well-defined job, which makes the code clearer and less prone to errors.

By following the single responsibility principle, Alex can be confident that changes to one class won't affect unrelated parts of the game. For instance, if Alex needs to modify how resources work, he only needs to update the `Resource` class. This change won't impact the `Player` class or any other part of the game. This separation of responsibilities makes the game easier to manage and less likely to break when changes are introduced.

As Alex breaks down his game into objects, he's also applying the principle of encapsulation. **Encapsulation** keeps the internal workings of each object hidden, protecting the data while providing access only through well-defined properties and methods. For instance, the `Player` class can govern how the player's score is changed by awarding a bonus when players collect resources through the `CollectResource` method. This ensures that other classes don't accidentally modify data in ways that could break the game. Rather than handling every detail all at once, Alex can focus on one object at a time, such as defining what a player can do or how resources are managed. This modular approach makes the game easier to maintain, improves scalability, and reduces errors.

Step 2. Plan the Solution

Alex decides to break the game down into its essential parts: players and resources. To do this, he'll create classes that represent these objects, where each object is responsible for handling its own data and actions. This approach will allow Alex to focus on one piece of the problem at a time, making the solution easier to manage. To represent these parts, Alex will create two classes:

- `Player`: This class will handle a player's attributes (like their name and score) and methods (like collecting resources).
- `Resource`: This class will represent the resources in the game, with attributes like type (e.g., "Wood" or "Stone") and the number of resources available.

These classes will allow Alex to create objects for players and resources, which can interact with each other. For example, a player will collect resources and increase their score based on the type and amount of the resource.

Class Diagrams

When designing classes, it's often helpful to visually represent the structure of a class using a **class diagram**. A class diagram shows the attributes (data) and methods (actions) of a class, as well as how different classes are related to each other.

In a typical class diagram, each class is represented as a box with three sections. The top section displays the class name, the middle section lists the attributes or data fields of the class, and the bottom section lists the methods of the class. Figure 2.1 is a basic class diagram for Alex's game, showing the relationship between the Player class and a Resource class. Each player can collect resources, which will increase their score. Everything in the diagram is marked as public, indicated by the plus sign (+) before each attribute and method. This means that these attributes and methods are usable from outside the class.

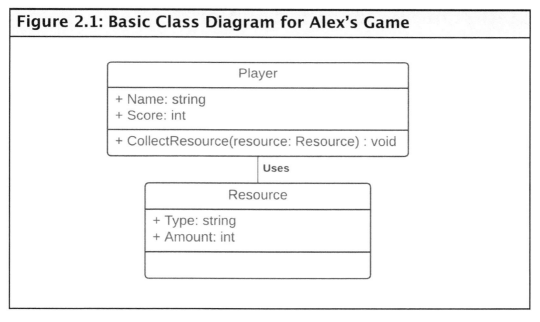

Figure 2.1: Basic Class Diagram for Alex's Game

In Alex's game world, players and resources each have their own unique attributes. The Player class includes two important details: the player's Name and their current Score. Meanwhile, the Resource class defines specific characteristics of the resources that players collect. For example, each resource has a Type, such as "Wood" or "Stone," and an Amount that indicates how many of those resources are available.

Players don't just passively interact with the game world; they actively collect resources. To handle this, Alex designed a method within the Player class called CollectResource. This method allows the player to collect resources by accepting a `Resource` object as an argument. As players encounter resources, the `CollectResource` method processes the interaction, allowing the game to update the player's score or resource count accordingly.

Finally, Alex recognized an important relationship between the `Player` and `Resource` classes: players need to interact with resources to collect them. The `Player` class relies on the existence of the `Resource` class, meaning that players "use" resources throughout the game to progress and earn points. This relationship is represented in the class diagram as a line connecting the two class boxes.

Step 3. Implement the Solution

Now that Alex has broken the problem down into smaller parts, it's time to write the code. Alex will start by creating a new file containing the `Resource` class, as shown in Code Block 2.1 below.

Code Block 2.1: Resource Class

```
1 | public class Resource
2 | {
3 |     public string Type { get; set; }
4 |     public int Amount { get; set; }
5 | }
```

Auto-Implemented Properties vs. Fields

In Chapter 1, we used a simple variable called `totalResources` to keep track of the resources collected in Alex's game. This variable was a **field**, which means it was directly storing the value of the total resources. Fields are useful when you need a simple way to store and access data, like a player's score or the total resources collected in the game.

However, as we build more complex programs, we'll use properties to handle data. While fields simply store data directly, properties give us more control over how data is managed in a class. With properties, we can make sure values are set correctly or changed only in certain ways. We can also hide the inner workings of how data is stored, which is a good practice in object-oriented programming (remember encapsulation?). Think of properties as a more powerful and flexible version of fields, giving us better control over our data as we create more complex programs.

Auto-implemented properties are a convenient way to create properties that allow us to get and set the values of certain attributes without writing extra code for validation or encapsulation logic at this stage. They act as a bridge between fields and methods, giving us more flexibility and control over how data is accessed and modified in the future.

Here's how auto-implemented properties work. Let's look at the Type and Amount attributes of the Resource class. In our game, each resource (like wood or stone) has a type and an amount. Rather than just using fields, Alex defined auto-implemented properties for these attributes in lines 3 and 4 in Code Block 2.1. They allow us to get (retrieve) the current value of the attribute, such as the type of resource or the amount, and they allow us to set (change) the value, such as updating the number of resources after a player collects some.

Next, Alex defines the Player class, as shown in Code Block 2.2. This class will manage each player's name, score, and the ability to collect resources.

Code Block 2.2: Player Class

```
1  public class Player
2  {
3      public string Name { get; set; }
4      public int Score { get; set; }
5
6      // Method for the player to collect a resource
7      public void CollectResource(Resource resource)
8      {
9          Score += resource.Amount;
10         Console.WriteLine($"{Name} collected {resource.Amount} units of
              {resource.Type}.");
11     }
12 }
```

In Alex's game world, each player is defined by two important characteristics: their Name and their Score. The player's Name represents their identity in the game, while the Score keeps track of how well they're performing by tallying up the total points they've accumulated as they collect resources and progress through the game.

The CollectResource method allows players to interact with resources in the game. Whenever a player collects a resource, the CollectResource method takes in that resource as an argument and adds the resource's amount to the player's current score. After updating the score, the method also prints a message to the console, letting the player know how many resources they've just collected and their updated score.

In this way, the CollectResource method ensures that every time a player gathers resources, the game updates their score and provides immediate feedback on their progress.

Step 4. Test the Solution

Now that Alex has both the Player and Resource classes, he can create player and resource objects that interact with each other. Let's walk through how Alex tests the interaction between a player and a resource.

Declaration vs. Instantiation

In object-oriented programming, we perform two key steps when creating an object: **declaration** and **instantiation**. Declaration tells the program what kind of object we want to work with (like a Player or a Resource), while instantiation creates an actual object of that type in memory. When we declare a variable, we tell the program what kind of object it is, and when we instantiate it, we give that variable a real object to work with.

In C#, we instantiate an object by using the new() keyword. The type of the object is declared on the left-hand side of the assignment, and the new() keyword is used on the right-hand side to assign a new instance of that type. Code Block 2.3 shows how Alex declares and instantiates a Player object (line 2) and a Resource object (line 7). He then uses the CollectResource method to simulate the player gathering resources in the game (line 12).

Code Block 2.3: Alex's Test Code

```
1| // Create a player object and set properties manually
2| Player player1 = new();
3| player1.Name = "Alex";
4| player1.Score = 0;
5|
6| // Create a resource object and set properties manually
7| Resource wood = new();
8| wood.Type = "Wood";
9| wood.Amount = 5;
10|
11| // Player collects the resource
12| player1.CollectResource(wood);
```

Let's break down what's happening in this test. Alex begins by declaring two variables: a `Player` object called `player1` (line 1a) and a `Resource` object called `wood` (line 7a). He then instantiates these objects using the `new()` keyword (lines 1a and 7b). This means that `player1` is a usable `Player` object that can store data and perform actions like collecting resources. Similarly, `wood` is a usable `Resource` object that can store a type and an amount.

Using the Dot Operator

Notice how Alex assigns values to the `Name` and `Score` properties of `player1` and the `Type` and `Amount` properties of `wood`. To do this, Alex uses the dot operator (`.`). The dot operator allows Alex to access the properties and methods of an object (not the class). For example:

- `player1.Name = "Alex";` assigns the name "Alex" to the `Name` property of the `player1` object.
- `wood.Type = "Wood";` sets the `Type` property of the `wood` object to "Wood".

It's important to remember that `Player` is the class (or type), and `player1` is the object (or instance) created from that class. We access the properties of objects like `player1` and `wood`, not the class itself, using the dot operator. So, we must write `player1.Name`, not `Player.Name`. The same applies to the `wood` object.

By using the dot operator, we can both retrieve (get) and modify (set) the values of an object's properties. In this case, Alex sets the properties manually to prepare the player and resource for interaction.

Simulating the Interaction

Once the properties are set, Alex calls the CollectResource method to simulate the player collecting the resource. The method is written to accept a Resource object as an argument, which in this case is the wood object. Inside the method, the player's Score is updated based on the amount of the resource collected, and a message is printed to the console to show the player's progress.

After running this test code, the player collects the wood, and their score increases by the amount of wood they gathered. The following message is displayed: Alex collected 5 units of Wood. This test successfully demonstrates the interaction between the Player and Resource classes. Alex now knows that when a player collects a resource, their score is updated, and the game provides immediate feedback. The instantiation process using new() ensures that objects are created and ready to interact with each other, while the dot operator makes it easy to access and modify their properties.

Step 5. Refine and Optimize

Once Alex confirms that the code works, the next step is to focus on optimizing it. One area for improvement is how objects are created and initialized. Currently, Alex must manually set the attributes (like Name, Score, Type, and Amount) after creating the objects. This approach not only introduces extra code, but also increases the risk that objects might be created in an incomplete or invalid state. For example, Alex could accidentally create a player object without setting a name, which could result in unexpected behavior or errors down the line. To avoid these pitfalls and ensure that objects are created in a valid state, Alex can use constructors.

Adding Constructors

A **constructor** is a special method that runs as an object is being instantiated, and its primary job is to safeguard the object's state by ensuring that critical properties are properly initialized. Unlike other methods, constructors do not have an explicit return type (not even `void`) because their job is to initialize the object itself (it may help to think of the constructor as implicitly returning an instance of the class, so C# already knows what type it will return). Another difference from other methods is that the name of the constructor must match the name of its class. Constructors allow the designer of a class to stipulate which attributes must be provided, ensuring that the object is fully and correctly initialized right from the start. This aligns with the principle of encapsulation, which gives the class the job of protecting its own internal state.

In C#, if no constructor is defined, the compiler automatically provides a default constructor. This constructor initializes all fields to their default values (e.g., 0 for numeric types, `'\0'` for `char`, and `null` for objects). While useful, default constructors don't offer the control necessary for initializing properties that have no logical default value, such as the player's name or a resource's type and amount. Allowing such fields to remain uninitialized could lead to incomplete or invalid objects that break the program logic.

On the other hand, certain attributes like score do have reasonable default values. For a new player, it makes sense to initialize the score to zero, so there's no need to include it as a parameter to the constructor. Code Block 2.4 and Code Block 2.5 show how Alex can use custom constructors in the `Player` and `Resource` classes to set a player's name and score or a resource's type and amount at the time the object is created. This approach improves the efficiency and readability of the code.

Code Block 2.4: Constructor for the Player Class

```
1  public class Player
2  {
3     public string Name { get; set; }
4     public int Score { get; set; }
5
6     // Player constructor
7     public Player(string playerName)
8     {
9       Name = playerName;
10      Score = 0;
11    }
```

(continued on next page) →

```
12|  → (continued from previous page)
13|
14|     // Method for the player to collect a resource
15|     public void CollectResource(Resource resource)
16|     {
17|       Score += resource.Amount;
18|       Console.WriteLine($"{Name} collected {resource.Amount} units of
    ↵    {resource.Type}.");
19|     }
20|  }
```

The Player class constructor now requires that Alex provide a name when creating a player, ensuring that the player object is never left in an invalid state. The score is automatically set to 0, because that is a reasonable default for new players.

Code Block 2.5: Constructor for the Resource Class

```
1|  public class Resource
2|  {
3|     public string Type { get; set; }
4|     public int Amount { get; set; }
5|
6|     // Resource constructor
7|     public Resource(string type, int amount)
8|     {
9|       Type = type;
10|       Amount = amount;
11|     }
12|  }
```

Similarly, the Resource constructor ensures that the resource's type and amount are provided when the object is created. Now that he has added constructors, Alex can create players and resources more efficiently and with guaranteed consistency, as shown in Code Block 2.6.

Code Block 2.6: Using Constructors to Instantiate Objects

```
1|  // Create a player object using the constructor
2|  Player player1 = new("Alex");
3|
4|  // Creating a resource object using the constructor
5|  Resource wood = new("Wood", 5);
6|
7|  // Player collects the resource
8|  player1.CollectResource(wood);
```

By using constructors, Alex ensures that key properties like Name, Type, and Amount are always initialized correctly, while Score defaults to a reasonable starting value. This approach helps safeguard the object's state, prevents invalid data, and makes the code both cleaner and more reliable. With constructors, Alex enhances the integrity of his objects and ensures that they are always in a valid state right from the moment they are created.

After making changes to the structure of the Player and Resource classes, Alex updates his class diagram in Figure 2.2 to reflect the latest modifications. Keeping documentation in sync with the code is an essential habit for any programmer. By regularly updating diagrams and documentation, problem-solvers ensure their design remains accurate and easy to understand as the project grows.

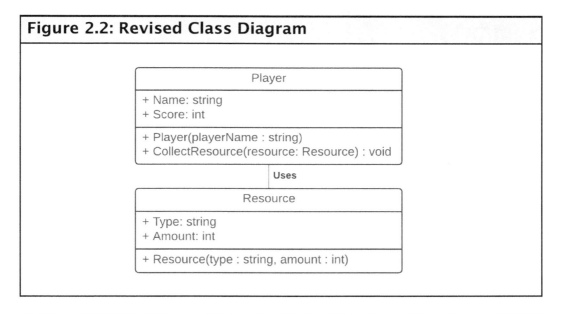

Figure 2.2: Revised Class Diagram

Recap: Breaking Down Big Problems

As Alex worked through this problem of designing a game where players collect resources and earn points, he applied the strategy of breaking down a large problem into smaller parts, which helped him focus on solving one piece of the problem at a time. By representing players and resources as objects, Alex was able to manage each part of the game's logic independently. Let's add this strategy to your growing problem-solving toolkit in Text Box 2.1.

Text Box 2.1: Problem–Solving Strategies

1. **Follow the Five-Step Problem-Solving Process**
   Understand the problem, plan the solution, implement the solution, test the solution, and finally refine and optimize it. This structured approach will help you systematically tackle any programming challenge you encounter.
2. **Break Down Big Problems into Smaller Parts**
   Whenever you face a large, complicated problem, break it down into smaller, simpler parts. In programming, this often involves using objects and classes to represent different pieces of the problem. By focusing on one piece at a time, you'll find the overall solution much easier to achieve.

Summary

In this chapter, we focused on the important concept of breaking down large problems into smaller, manageable parts. We learned that in programming, as in life, tackling a complex problem becomes easier when we divide it into its individual components. This strategy lies at the heart of object-oriented programming (OOP), where we model real-world problems by creating classes and objects.

Using Alex's game world, we demonstrated how to split the larger task of tracking player progress into smaller steps, like creating Player and Resource classes. These classes have attributes, which are managed through auto-implemented properties.

We also introduced constructors, which allow us to initialize objects when they are created. By defining constructors in the Player and Resource classes, Alex can set initial values for his objects as soon as they are created, making the code more resistant to errors later on.

A key tool in object-oriented programming is the dot operator, which allows us to access and modify the properties of objects. Alex used this operator to set a player's name, adjust their score, and interact with the game's resources. Additionally, we saw how objects, like players and resources, can interact with one another to solve specific tasks, such as updating the player's score when they collect resources.

Ultimately, this chapter reinforced the idea that by breaking down big problems, like designing a game world, into smaller, more manageable pieces, we can approach complex programming challenges with confidence and clarity.

Review Questions

1. What is the importance of breaking down a large problem into smaller, more manageable parts in both programming and life? Can you think of an example outside of coding where this approach would be beneficial?

2. Explain in your own words how object-oriented programming (OOP) helps to organize code and solve problems. How does this method relate to the problem-solving process introduced in Chapter 1?

3. How can thinking about programming in terms of objects (such as players and resources) help simplify a complex task like game design? What are some real-world objects you could model in a program?

4. What is encapsulation, and why might this concept be important for writing maintainable code?

5. What is the difference between an attribute and a method in a class? How do these two concepts work together to define a class?

6. How does the problem-solving strategy of breaking down problems align with biblical stewardship? How can approaching code in this way help you be a better steward of your time and resources?

7. Describe what auto-implemented properties are and explain their purpose. Why would you use them in a class?

8. What do you think the role of faith might be in helping you solve complex challenges, whether in programming or in everyday life? How might applying biblical principles influence the way you approach coding or problem-solving in general?

9. What is a constructor in a class, and why would you use one? Explain the difference between a constructor with parameters and a constructor without parameters.

Practice Problems

1. Create a class diagram for a Book class for a library system. The Book class should have the following attributes and method:

   Title: A string representing the book's title.

   Author: A string representing the author's name.

   Pages: An integer representing the number of pages in the book

   DisplayInfo(): A method that prints the book's title, author, and number of pages.

2. Create a class diagram for a BankAccount class for a banking application. The BankAccount class should have the following attributes and method:

   AccountNumber: A string representing the account number.

   Balance: A decimal number representing the current account balance.

   AccountHolder: A string representing the name of the account holder.

   Deposit(amount): A method that adds the amount to the account balance.

3. Create a class diagram that shows the relationship between the Vehicle class and the Engine class. Include the following attributes and methods for both classes and show the relationship between them.

   a. Vehicle Class:

      i. Make: A string representing the car's make (e.g., Toyota).

      ii. Model: A string representing the car's model (e.g., Camry).

      iii. Year: An integer representing the car's year.

      iv. Engine: A reference to the Engine class, representing that each vehicle has an engine

      v. DisplayDetails(): A method that displays the car's make, model, and year.

   b. Engine Class:

      i. Horsepower: An integer representing the engine's horsepower.

      ii. Type: A string representing the type of engine (e.g., "V6").

4. Create a class diagram that shows the relationship between the Author and Book classes. Include the following attributes and methods for both classes and show the relationship between them.

   Author Class:

   iii. Name: A string representing the author's name (e.g., "C.S. Lewis").

   iv. Nationality: A string representing the author's nationality (e.g., "British").

   v. DisplayAuthorInfo(): A method that prints the author's name and nationality.

   a. Book Class:

   i. Title: A string representing the book's title.

   ii. Pages: An integer representing the number of pages in the book.

   iii. Author: A reference to the Author class, meaning that each book has one author.

5. Based on the class diagram that you created in Problem 1 for the Book class, write the C# code that defines the Book class. Be sure to include the Title, Author, and Pages attributes, and implement the DisplayInfo() method, which prints the book's information.

   Example Output:

   ```
   Book Title: Mere Christianity
   Author: C.S. Lewis
   Pages: 227
   ```

6. Using the class diagram that you created in Problem 2 for the BankAccount class, write the C# code that defines the BankAccount class. Be sure to include the AccountNumber, Balance, and AccountHolder attributes. Implement the Deposit() method, which increases the balance by the specified amount.

   Example Output:

   ```
   Deposit of $200 successful.
   New balance: $1,200.
   ```

7. Based on the class diagram that you created in Problem 3 for the Vehicle and Engine classes, write the C# code that defines both classes. Ensure that each Vehicle object contains a reference to an Engine object. Implement the DisplayDetails() method to display the car's make, model, year, and engine details.

Example Output:

```
Vehicle: Toyota Camry (2015)
Engine: V6 with 270 horsepower
```

8. Based on the class diagram that you created in Problem 4 for the Author and Book classes, write the C# code that defines both classes. Ensure that each Book object contains a reference to an Author object. Implement the DisplayAuthorInfo() method to display the author's information.

Example Output:

```
Author: C.S. Lewis (British)
Book: Mere Christianity, 227 pages
```

"The beginning of wisdom is this: Get wisdom,
and whatever you get, get insight."
Proverbs 4:7 (ESV)

CHAPTER 3

MAKING DECISIONS IN CODE

Introduction

As Christians, we recognize that decision-making is a critical part of our God-given role as His image bearers. As we saw in Chapter 1, the dominion mandate (Genesis 1:28) calls us to exercise wise stewardship and responsible decision-making. As God's representatives on earth, we are entrusted with the responsibility to choose wisely and consider the impact of our decisions, evaluate their consequences, and act with care and integrity.

Making wise decisions goes beyond merely processing information or predicting outcomes. As Proverbs 4:7 (ESV) reminds us, "The beginning of wisdom is this: Get wisdom, and whatever you get, get insight." We are called to align our choices with God's truth, exercising both wisdom and discernment. This principle applies not only in life but also in programming, where careful decision-making ensures reliability and excellence.

In life, as in programming, quality decision-making requires more than a surface-level understanding of the situation. It demands deep consideration of the consequences, the potential for error, and the need for wisdom in choosing the best path. Proverbs 22:3 (ESV) reminds us, "The prudent sees danger and hides himself, but the simple go on and suffer for it." This means not only evaluating the information we have but also seeking to ensure that our choices align with God's principles of truth, goodness, and excellence.

When we write code, we must bring this same level of intentionality to the decisions we make. The quality of those decisions, such as how wisely we choose to handle different scenarios, ultimately determines whether our program will be reliable and effective. Most importantly, the work we do in writing code is an act of worship as we seek to do all things for God's glory (1 Corinthians 10:31).

In this chapter, we'll explore how Alex uses decision structures to ensure that his game responds appropriately to player input. In the same way that we are called to make wise choices in life, we'll see how Alex approaches decision-making thoughtfully, planning for every possible scenario to ensure the game runs correctly. We'll use the same five-step problem-solving process introduced in Chapter 1 to explore how to make these thoughtful decisions using structures like if-else and switch statements in Alex's game.

Step 1. Understand the Problem

In Alex's game world, players collect resources, and based on certain conditions, they may receive rewards. To achieve this, Alex needs the game to make decisions dynamically, depending on the player's progress. For instance, the game must check how many resources a player has collected and decide whether to give them a score bonus.

When making decisions in code, it's important to account not only for the typical inputs but also for boundary cases. **Boundary cases** or **edge cases** are extreme values that might cause errors or unexpected behavior. Ignoring these edge cases can undermine the program's stability. For example, Alex wants his game to reward players for collecting resources, so he will need to identify the appropriate minimum and maximum number of resources that are possible. Those minimum and maximum values would be the boundary cases. Values outside of those boundaries could cause problems for his game, unless he plans for those possibilities early in the problem-solving process. For example, Alex will need to decide what happens when a player collects exactly 0 resources, or what happens if they input a negative value? Boundary cases are just as important to handle as the typical scenarios.

Step 2. Plan the Solution

In many programming challenges, we're faced with the need to evaluate several possible conditions to decide on the correct action. This is where an important problem-solving strategy comes into play, called Evaluating Multiple Scenarios. This strategy ensures that our code is prepared to handle a wide range of inputs by considering all the possible conditions it might encounter. By systematically evaluating all the possible scenarios, we ensure that our code responds to each potential outcome in a thoughtful and reliable way. Evaluating Multiple Scenarios involves three main steps. First, identify the typical inputs or situations the program will handle. Second, consider the edge or boundary cases, and identify specific values just below, exactly at, and just above the boundary points. Third, determine the best course of action for each test value to ensure the program behaves appropriately under all circumstances.

For example, in Alex's game world, players collect resources, and the game must decide what happens based on how many resources a player has collected. Alex identifies the following typical inputs: fewer than 50 resources, between 50 and 99 resources, and 100 or more resources. Alex next plans for the edge or boundary cases to prevent his game from producing errors. Here are the important boundary cases Alex needs to consider:

- **Minimum boundary**: Alex identifies the minimum boundary case as zero resources. He then selects values below the boundary, at the boundary, and just above the boundary for consideration. For example, what happens if the player enters a negative number for collected resources? Should this be allowed, or should the game give an error or warning? What if the player collects 0 resources? Should the game encourage them to collect more? What should happen if the player only enters 1 resource? Should this have the same response as a player who collects 20 resources?

- **Halfway boundary**: Alex identifies another boundary at the halfway mark of 50 resources. What if the player collects 49 resources? What if they collect exactly 50? Or what if the player collects 51 resources? Should the game give different feedback to the player?

- **Maximum boundary**: Alex identifies a final boundary at the number of resources needed for a score bonus, 100. What if the player collects 99 resources, or what if the player collects exactly 100 resources? What should happen if the player collects more than 100 resources? Should there be a limit to the amount of the score bonus the player can receive beyond 100?

By following the Evaluating Multiple Scenarios strategy and the Break Down Large Problems strategy, Alex can divide up these situations and plan for each one, ensuring that the game responds correctly. Let's walk through Alex's decisions for each of the different scenarios:

- **Scenario 1 (Negative Values)**: If the player enters a negative number of resources, the game should give a clear error message or warning. Negative numbers don't make sense in this context and allowing them could break the game logic.

- **Scenario 2 (0)**: If the player collects exactly 0 resources, they should not receive a score bonus. The game should instead acknowledge the fact that they have not collected anything yet.

- **Scenario 3 (1 to 49)**: If the player collects between 1 and 49 resources, they should not receive a score bonus. The game should instead encourage the player to collect more resources to earn a bonus.

- **Scenario 4 (50)**: If the player collects between 50 and 99 resources, the game should acknowledge their progress and motivate them to continue collecting.
- **Scenario 5 (100)**: If the player collects 100 or more resources, they earn a score bonus equal to the number of resources they collected, even if the number of resources collected exceeds 100.

To clarify his plan, Alex writes out the logic using pseudo-code. Text Box 3.1 shows Alex's pseudo-code for handling these scenarios. By writing this pseudo-code, Alex can outline the logic for each **condition** in a straightforward way. He can also add this pseudo-code as comments in his code editor, which provides a clear structure for the code he will write later. Starting with pseudo-code helps Alex stay organized and ensures he doesn't miss any steps.

Text Box 3.1: Pseudo-code

If number of resources collected is less than 0
    Display "Error: Count cannot be negative."
Otherwise if the number of resources collected is greater than or equal to 100
    Add number of resources collected to score
    Display "Congratulations! You earned a bonus."
Otherwise if the number of resources collected is greater than or equal to 50
    Display "Good job! You're halfway there."
Otherwise if the number of resources collected is equal to 0
    Display "No resources collected."
Otherwise
    Display "Keep collecting to reach your goal."

To visually represent this decision-making process, Alex also creates an activity diagram, as shown in Figure 3.1, to match the pseudo-code. The activity diagram starts with an initial node, which marks the beginning of the program's flow. Each decision point is represented by a diamond shape, symbolizing a branching moment in the flow. Prior to each diamond, an activity rectangle is used to identify the condition that is evaluated in the following diamond.

The outputs from the diamond represent the possible outcomes: either yes or no (or true or false). For example, the diagram branches at the first decision point, where it checks if the resources collected were

Figure 3.1: Activity Diagram

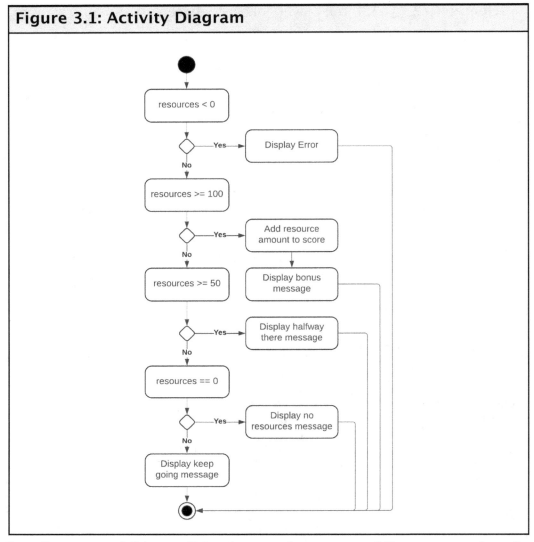

less than zero. If this condition is true, the program follows one path and displays an error message. If the condition is false, the program moves on to the next decision point. This use of diamonds allows Alex to visually track the different paths that the program will take based on the result of each condition, making it clear how each scenario is handled within the program's flow.

By using both pseudo-code and an activity diagram, Alex gains a deeper understanding of the logic required for his game, ensuring that he has thoroughly planned for primary and boundary cases. The pseudo-code provides a clear, step-by-step outline of the actions, while the activity diagram offers a visual representation of the program's flow, highlighting the decision points and branching paths. Together, these tools help Alex verify that he has covered all possible scenarios, including edge cases where players might provide unexpected inputs.

It's important to note, however, that not every problem requires both tools. For simpler problems, pseudo-code might be the optimal choice, as it offers a straightforward way to outline the code. For problems with more complex flows, an activity diagram can better illustrate the branching paths and decision points. Ultimately, the choice depends on the complexity of the problem and the level of detail required. By thoughtfully selecting the right planning tool, Alex ensures that his game is robust, adaptable, and free from errors arising from unanticipated situations.

Step 3: Implement the Solution

Now that Alex has carefully planned his solution, considering both the primary scenarios and boundary cases, he's ready to implement the code. Code Block 3.1 shows Alex's updated Player class.

Alex knows the game needs to evaluate how many resources a player has collected and provide the appropriate feedback based on their progress. To manage situations like this in programming, we use decision structures, called the if statement. These structures evaluate specific conditions, and they determine which block of code to execute based on whether the condition is true or false.

Alex writes his if structure, ensuring that his game handles both typical cases and boundary case inputs. Alex starts by considering the possibility of invalid inputs, specifically, negative values. In line 15, he writes a condition to check if the player enters a negative number of resources. If the resource amount is negative, the game will not update the player's score, and it will display an error message to inform the player that resource counts can't be negative (line 17).

For players who collect 100 or more resources (line 19), Alex chooses to reward them with a score bonus equal to the number of resources they

Code Block 3.1: Updated Player Class with Decision-Making

```
 1| public class Player
 2| {
 3|    public string Name { get; set; }
 4|    public int Score { get; set; }
 5|
 6|    public Player(string playerName)
 7|    {
 8|      Name = playerName;
 9|      Score = 0;
10|    }
11|
12|    public void CollectResource(Resource resource)
13|    {
14|      // Decision logic based on the collected resources
15|      if (resource.Amount < 0)
16|      {
17|        Console.WriteLine("Error: Count cannot be negative.");
18|      }
19|      else if (resource.Amount >= 100)
20|      {
21|        Score += resource.Amount;
22|        Console.WriteLine("You earned a score bonus!");
23|      }
24|      else if (resource.Amount >= 50)
25|      {
26|        Console.WriteLine("Good job! You're halfway there.");
27|      }
28|      else if (resource.Amount == 0)
29|      {
30|        Console.WriteLine("No resources collected.");
31|      }
32|      else
33|      {
34|        Console.WriteLine("Keep going to reach your goal.");
35|      }
36|    }
37| }
```

collected (line 21). This encourages players to push toward higher milestones and gives them positive feedback for their progress (line 22).

But what if the player hasn't collected 100 resources? Alex realizes that halfway points are important markers of progress, and he wants the players to stay motivated on their journey toward the bonus. For players who have made decent progress but aren't quite there yet, Alex writes another condition to check if the player has collected between 50 and 99 resources. To do this, he uses the condition in line 24. At first glance, it may seem like this condition only checks whether the player has collected 50 resources or more, so where's the boundary for 99?

Here's where the if-else structure comes into play. The earlier condition in line 19 already captures all players who have collected 100 or more resources. That means once the program reaches the condition in line 24, it's only considering players who have fewer than 100 resources. This is because if a player had 100 or more, the first if block would have already executed, and the program wouldn't check the else if block. So effectively, this range covers the players who are at least halfway toward their bonus, and the game encourages them to keep going (line 26).

Of course, Alex doesn't forget about the players who haven't started collecting resources yet. For those who have collected exactly 0 resources (line 28), he displays a message indicating nothing has been collected yet (line 30). This way, even the players who haven't contributed anything to their resource collection still receive a message, encouraging them to start gathering resources.

Finally, Alex adds a default message for all other cases (line 34), where players have collected between 1 and 49 resources. This message encourages the players to continue collecting resources, letting them know they're on their way to reaching the next goal.

In crafting this decision structure, Alex makes sure to account for a wide range of possible inputs, from negative values to high scores. By planning for both the typical and edge cases, Alex ensures that the game is responsive and user-friendly. The if structure he's written not only helps the game run correctly but also gives players an interactive experience that adapts to their progress.

Boolean Operators

In many programming challenges, especially those involving decision-making, we often need to evaluate multiple conditions simultaneously to determine the correct course of action. Sometimes a single condition isn't enough; we need to combine two or more conditions to make a more nuanced decision. This is where boolean operators come into play. Boolean operators, such as && (AND) and || (OR), let us combine multiple conditions into a single decision structure. This allows for more nuanced checks without adding extra if statements.

Let's go back to Alex's game. In some situations, he may want to provide more specific feedback when a player's resource count falls within a narrower range. For example, what if Alex wanted the game to display a different message if the player collected between 70 and 79 resources? Code Block 3.2 shows how Alex could use boolean operators to handle this.

Code Block 3.2: Boolean AND Operator

```
1  if (resource.Amount >= 70 && resource.Amount <= 79)
2  {
3    Console.WriteLine("Good job! You're almost there.");
4  }
```

In this example, Alex uses the && operator to check for two conditions at the same time. The condition in line 1 ensures that only players who have collected between 70 and 79 resources receive the message. The && operator means both conditions must be true for this block of code to run. In this case, the player must have collected at least 70 resources *and* fewer than 79 for the game to display "Good job! You're almost there."

If Alex wanted to display a message to players who collect exactly 98 *or* exactly 99 resources, he can use the code shown in Code Block 3.3. The == operator is used to make an exact comparison, and the || operator, ensures that the block of code will execute if *either* condition is true.

Code Block 3.3: Boolean OR operator

```
1  if (resource.Amount == 98 || resource.Amount == 99)
2  {
3    Console.WriteLine("You are so close!");
4  }
```

In more complex decision-making situations, you might need to combine both && and || in the same statement. For example, suppose Alex wants to reward players who either collect between 100 *and* 150 resources, *or* players who collect exactly 200 resources. He can combine these conditions using both operators to account for these specific cases, as shown in Code Block 3.4.

Code Block 3.4: Complex Boolean Conditions

```
1  if ((resource.Amount >= 100 && resource.Amount <= 150) ||
   ↳    resource.Amount == 200)
2  {
3      Console.WriteLine("Special bonus awarded!");
4  }
```

In this example, both && and || work together. The first part of the condition (line 1) checks if the player has collected between 100 and 150 resources, while the second part (line 2) checks if the player has collected exactly 200 resources. If either of these conditions is true, the block of code that displays the message will run. Combining operators this way allows us to handle more complex scenarios efficiently.

By using boolean operators effectively, Alex can introduce more flexibility and control into his decision-making structures. These operators allow him to handle more complex scenarios within the game without writing additional if statements. For example, Alex could easily extend this logic to check for other milestones, such as rewarding players at multiple levels of resource collection or combining conditions for special rewards when players hit certain targets. This ensures that the game remains engaging and that players receive accurate feedback, whether they're just getting started, reaching key milestones, or surpassing significant thresholds.

The ability to combine multiple conditions is a powerful tool in decision-making, allowing Alex to refine the game's logic in ways that make it more interactive and personalized for players. It also reinforces the concept that making wise decisions in programming involves not just handling the typical cases but carefully considering the different combinations of inputs that might affect the program's behavior.

Step 4. Test the Solution

When testing decision structures, it's important to test not only the typical cases but also the boundary cases, including edge cases like negative inputs. This helps us verify that our program works correctly for a wide range of possible values and handles unexpected inputs gracefully. Alex knows that players could potentially input invalid or extreme values, and he wants to ensure the game responds correctly in each scenario. Code Block 3.5 lists Alex's test code.

Code Block 3.5: Alex's Decision Test Code

```
1  // Create a player object
2  Player player1 = new("Alex");
3
4  // Test Case 1: resource.Amount = -5
5  Resource negativeResources = new("Stone", -5);
6  player1.CollectResource(negativeResources);
7  Console.WriteLine($"Player Score: {player1.Score}\n");
8  // Expected Output: "Error: Count cannot be negative."
9  // Expected Score: 0 (no change)
10
11 // Test Case 2: resource.Amount = 0
12 Resource zeroResources = new("Wood", 0);
13 player1.CollectResource(zeroResources);
14 Console.WriteLine($"Player Score: {player1.Score}\n");
15 // Expected Output: "No resources collected."
16 // Expected Score: 0 (no change)
17
18 // Test Case 3: resource.Amount = 50
19 Resource fiftyResources = new("Iron", 50);
20 player1.CollectResource(fiftyResources);
21 Console.WriteLine($"Player Score: {player1.Score}\n");
22 // Expected Output: "Good job! You're halfway there."
23 // Expected Score: 0 (no change)
24
25 // Test Case 4: resource.Amount = 99
26 Resource ninetyNineResources = new("Gold", 99);
27 player1.CollectResource(ninetyNineResources);
28 Console.WriteLine($"Player Score: {player1.Score}\n");
29 // Expected Output: "Good job! You're halfway there."
30 // Expected Score: 0 (no change)
31
32 // Test Case 5: resource.Amount = 100 Resource
33 Resource hundredResources = new("Diamond", 100);
34 player1.CollectResource(hundredResources);
35 Console.WriteLine($"Player Score: {player1.Score}\n");
36 // Expected Output: "You earned a score bonus!"
37 // Expected Score: 100 (score updated)
```

Test Case 1 (lines 4-9) checks how the program handles negative input, ensuring that invalid data is caught, and the score remains unaffected. Test Case 2 (lines 11-16) tests the minimum boundary condition by trying to collect 0 resources, verifying that the correct message is displayed and that no changes are made to the player's score. Test Cases 3 (lines 18-23) and 4 (lines 25-30) verify how the program handles mid-range resource inputs, specifically testing the boundary of 50 and the upper limit of 99. These tests confirm that the correct messages are displayed for players in this range without affecting the player's score. Test Case 5 (lines 32-37) ensures that the program handles the exact case of 100 resources, testing whether the correct message is displayed, and the score is updated as expected.

By testing these typical, boundary cases, Alex ensures that the decision structure works as expected, no matter what value the player provides. Thorough testing helps verify that the game responds correctly at every edge of the input spectrum, allowing for a more robust and user-friendly gaming experience.

Step 5. Refine and Optimize

After testing his initial code, Alex realizes that while the logic works well, there's still room for improvement. Specifically, he notices that his `CollectResource` method must handle some basic data validation, like checking if the number of resources collected is negative. This kind of validation is essential, but it clutters up the main game logic. Alex decides to streamline the code by moving this validation into the `Resource` class itself, using full properties.

Full Properties for Data Validation

A **full property** allows Alex to control how data is set or retrieved in a class. Rather than simply storing a value directly, a full property includes a custom getter and setter that can perform checks or transformations on the data. By adding a full property to the `Resource` class, Alex can ensure that only valid resource amounts are accepted from the start. This way, he doesn't need to repeatedly check for negative values in every method that interacts with resources. Instead, the validation logic is centralized in the property, making the code cleaner and easier to maintain.

In Code Block 3.6, Alex uses a full property for `Amount` in the `Resource` class. A full property includes both a get and a set accessor, allowing Alex to customize what happens when the property is read or assigned a new value. The getter allows other parts of the program to retrieve the current value of `Amount`, while the setter defines specific rules whenever a new value is assigned to it. In this case, the setter checks if the incoming value is negative. If so, it sets Amount to zero and displays an error message, ensuring that Amount cannot hold an invalid value. This way, any time the Amount property is set, whether it's from the CollectResource method or any other part of the game, it will automatically enforce this rule.

Code Block 3.6: Resource Class with Full Property for Amount

```
 1| public class Resource
 2| {
 3|    public string Type { get; set; }
 4|    private int amount; // Backing field for the Amount property
 5|    public int Amount
 6|    {
 7|      get { return amount; }
 8|      set
 9|      {
10|        if (value < 0)
11|        {
12|          Console.WriteLine("Error: Setting amount to 0.");
13|          amount = 0;
14|        }
15|        else
16|        {
17|          amount = value;
18|        }
19|      }
20|    }
21|
22|    public Resource(string type, int initialAmount)
23|    {
24|      Type = type;
25|      Amount = initialAmount; // Uses the property, not the field
26|    }
27| }
```

This code highlights the contrast between auto-implemented properties and full properties with a backing field. The Type property, for instance, is an **auto-implemented property**. The code in line 3 is a shorthand that allows C# to automatically create a hidden backing field to store the value. Auto-implemented properties are ideal for cases where you don't need any special logic to handle the value, so Type simply stores and retrieves a string without any additional processing or validation.

On the other hand, the Amount property is defined as a full property with a custom getter and setter. In line 4, Alex explicitly declares a private backing field called amount to store the actual value, and he uses the get and set accessors to control how this value is accessed and modified. When the property is accessed (using get), it simply returns the current value of the backing field amount. However, when the property is assigned a new value (using set), the setter first performs a check to see if the new value, represented by the keyword, value, is negative. If it is, the setter displays an error message and assigns zero to amount, effectively resetting it. If the value is non-negative, the setter assigns the value directly to amount.

If Alex were willing to remove the error message to the user, he could streamline his code even further, using a ternary operator. A **ternary operator** is a quick and compact way to make decisions in code, where instead of using a full if-else statement, you can decide between two values on one line. It works like this: you start with a condition followed by a question mark (?), then the value you want to return if the condition is true, followed by a colon (:), and finally the value to return if the condition is false. For example, condition ? valueIfTrue : valueIfFalse. Code Block 3.7 shows how Alex might refine the Amount property using a ternary operator.

Code Block 3.7: Using the Ternary Operator

```
 1  public class Resource
 2  {
 3     public string Type { get; set; }
 4
 5     private int amount; // Backing field for the Amount property
 6
 7     public int Amount
 8     {
 9       get
10       {
11         return amount;
12       }
13       set
14       {
15         amount = value < 0 ? 0 : value;
16       }
17     }
18
19     public Resource(string type, int initialAmount)
20     {
21       Type = type;
22       Amount = initialAmount; // Uses the property, not the field
23     }
24  }
```

By using a backing field, Alex gains finer control over how data is stored and validated. This allows him to enforce rules on the Amount property that are applied consistently throughout the program, regardless of where or how the property is modified. This approach aligns with the concept of data encapsulation, where the property controls access to the private backing field, ensuring that only valid data is stored. In this way, full properties enable Alex to protect the internal state of his class and ensure that only valid data is stored, especially in scenarios where properties represent critical game elements like resources.

With the validation logic now inside the Amount property, the CollectResource method can focus solely on the game mechanics. It no longer needs to handle data validation for the resource amount, since that logic is taken care of by the Resource class itself. The updated CollectResource method in Code Block 3.8 becomes more concise and focused on what happens when a player collects a resource, rather than also validating the data.

Code Block 3.8: Revised CollectResource Method

```
 1| public class Player
 2| {
 3|     public string Name { get; set; }
 4|     public int Score { get; set; }
 5|
 6|     public Player(string playerName)
 7|     {
 8|         Name = playerName;
 9|         Score = 0;
10|     }
11|     public void CollectResource(Resource resource)
12|     {
13|         // Decision logic based on the collected resources
14|         if (resource.Amount >= 100)
15|         {
16|             Score += resource.Amount;
17|             Console.WriteLine("You earned a score bonus!");
18|         }
19|         else if (resource.Amount >= 50)
20|         {
21|             Console.WriteLine("Good job! You're halfway there.");
22|         }
23|         else if (resource.Amount == 0)
24|         {
25|             Console.WriteLine("No resources collected.");
26|         }
27|         else
28|         {
29|             Console.WriteLine("Keep going to reach your goal.");
30|         }
31|     }
32| }
```

This optimization step demonstrates that improving code isn't always about making it faster; sometimes, it's about making it smarter and more reliable. Full properties help Alex take his game a step closer to being well-designed and maintainable, which are qualities that reflect the thoughtfulness and diligence we should strive for in our code.

Optimizing with Switch

After testing this revised code, Alex realizes that while the if-else structure works well for checking different ranges of resources, it can be simplified. Since all the conditions are based on the same variable, Alex can change to a switch statement to streamline the code.

Code Block 3.9: The switch Statement

```
public class Player
{
  public string Name { get; set; }
  public int Score { get; set; }

  public Player(string playerName)
  {
    Name = playerName;
    Score = 0;
  }

  public void CollectResource(Resource resource)
  {
    // Decision logic based on the collected resources
    switch (resource.Amount)
    {
      case >= 100:
        Score += resource.Amount;
        Console.WriteLine("You earned a score bonus!");
        break;
      case >= 50:
        Console.WriteLine("Good job! You're halfway there.");
        break;

      case 0:
        Console.WriteLine("No resources collected.");
        break;
      default:
        Console.WriteLine("Keep going to reach your goal.");
        break;
    }
  }
}
```

A **switch statement** is an ideal choice when evaluating a single variable against multiple conditions. It reduces repetition by avoiding multiple checks of the same variable and makes the code easier to read.

Each `case` in a `switch` represents a specific condition, and the `break` keyword is used to exit the switch once the code for that condition has been executed. Without the `break` keyword, the program would continue executing subsequent cases, a behavior known as "fall-through." While fall-through can sometimes be useful, such as when grouping cases together, it is often unintended and can lead to errors if not handled carefully. The `default` case, which is optional, acts as a catch-all for any values not explicitly handled by the other cases. Code Block 3.9 shows the updated code using a `switch` statement.

The default case (line 28) handles all values that don't meet the previous conditions, covering scenarios where the player has collected between 1 and 49 resources. By changing to this approach, Alex simplifies his coding logic, making it easier to read, maintain, and scale as the game grows in complexity.

Recap: Evaluate Multiple Scenarios

As Alex worked through this problem, he applied the problem-solving strategy of Evaluating Multiple Scenarios to design a game where players collect resources and earn points. By carefully considering the range of possible situations, including typical cases as well as boundary and edge cases, Alex was able to ensure that his game responded appropriately to different inputs. This strategy involves identifying all the conditions that might impact the program's behavior, allowing Alex to make purposeful decisions on how the game should react to each scenario. Let's add Evaluating Multiple Scenarios to your growing problem-solving toolkit in Text Box 3.2.

Summary

In this chapter, we explored how to make decisions in programming using the `if` and `else if` structures, which allow us to control the flow of our code based on specific conditions. We also introduced the concept of boundary cases, which are critical edge values that must be tested to ensure the robustness of our decision structures. By planning for these boundary cases, we can create code that behaves correctly across a wide range of inputs. Additionally, we applied the Evaluating Multiple Scenarios problem-solving strategy to develop resilient and thoughtful solutions. We also introduced full properties as an optimization technique, emphasizing that making wise decisions isn't just about achieving desired functionality; it's also about writing code that is maintainable, reliable, and aligned with best practices. Finally, we examined the `switch` statement, which simplifies decision-making by reducing repetition and improving code readability. We also covered key aspects of its syntax, including the `break` keyword and case fall-through, emphasizing its role in writing clean and maintainable code.

Text Box 3.2: Problem–Solving Strategies

1. **Follow the Five-Step Problem-Solving Process**
   Understand the problem, plan the solution, implement the solution, test the solution, and finally refine and optimize it. This structured approach will help you systematically tackle any programming challenge you encounter.

2. **Break Down Big Problems into Smaller Parts**
   Whenever you face a large, complicated problem, break it down into smaller, simpler parts. In programming, this often involves using objects and classes to represent different pieces of the problem. By focusing on one piece at a time, you'll find the overall solution much easier to achieve.

3. **Evaluate Multiple Scenarios**
   Plan for different conditions and map out the appropriate actions for each. This includes identifying the extreme values at the edges of the expected inputs and testing how the program behaves under these conditions.

Review Questions

1. Why is decision-making a critical part of programming, and how does it reflect our God-given role as His image bearers?

2. Explain the difference between typical cases and boundary cases in programming. Why is it important to account for both when writing decision structures?

3. What are some examples of boundary cases that need to be considered when determining rewards or outcomes in a game or application you might design?

4. What is the purpose of the if-else structure. How does it contrast with the switch structure?

5. What are boolean operators, and how can they be used to combine multiple conditions within a decision structure? Provide an example from a game or application you might design.

6. How does the switch syntax improve readability and conciseness when handling multiple conditions based on a single variable?

7. In what situations might a switch statement be more efficient than an if-else structure? Provide a scenario where you could benefit from using a switch statement in a game or application you might design.

8. What is a full property, and how does it differ from an auto-implemented property? Describe a scenario where using a full property is beneficial, especially in terms of ensuring data integrity in a program.

9. What are some advantages of using boolean operators (such as && and ||) in decision-making, and how do they differ from using multiple if-else statements?

10. How can full properties be used to enforce specific rules or constraints on the data being stored in an object? Provide an example of a class where a full property might be used to restrict invalid values and explain the impact this has on the program's reliability.

Practice Problems

1. **Check Voting Eligibility**: Write a program that asks the user for their age and displays a message indicating whether they are eligible to vote. Test boundary cases such as 17 and 18 to ensure the program handles them correctly.

2. **Categorize Grades**: Write a program that asks the user for a test score between 0 and 100. Use an if-else structure to print the

letter grade (A, B, C, D, or F) based on the score. Make sure to test boundary cases like -1, 59, 60, 69, 70, 79, 80, and 101.

3. **Difficulty Level**: Write a program that asks the user to enter a number representing the difficulty level (1 for Easy, 2 for Normal, 3 for Hard). Use a switch statement and test both valid and invalid inputs (e.g., 1, 2, 3, and 5).

4. **Even or Odd**: Write a program that asks the user for a number and uses an if-else statement to print whether the number is even or odd. If you need a hint, the modulus operator in C# (%) will calculate the remainder of a division problem. Even numbers will always have a remainder of 0 when divided by 2. Test boundary cases such as 0 and negative numbers.

5. **Categorize Grades with Switch**: Rewrite the program in Problem 2, using a switch statement instead of an if-else structure. Make sure to test boundary cases like -1, 59, 60, 69, 70, 79, 80, and 101.

6. **Person**: Create a Person class that has a property called Age. The Age property should be a full property with a private backing field called age. The set logic should ensure that age cannot be set to a negative number. If a negative number is attempted, the setter should set the age to 0 and print a message saying, "Age cannot be negative. Setting to 0." The get logic should return the value of the age backing field.

7. **Bank Account**: Create a BankAccount class with a property called Balance. Use a full property with a private backing field called balance. The set logic should ensure that balance does not go below a minimum of $50. If a value lower than $50 is attempted, it should print a message saying, "Balance cannot be set below $50," and not change the balance. Include get logic that returns the current balance.

"And these words that I command you today shall be on your heart. You shall teach them diligently to your children, and shall talk of them when you sit in your house, and when you walk by the way, and when you lie down, and when you rise."
Deuteronomy 6:6-7 (ESV)

CHAPTER 4

REPETITION WITH PURPOSE

Introduction

Repetition is a foundational aspect of Christian growth and maturity. God uses repetition in our lives to shape our character, refine our faith, and build spiritual resilience. For example, daily prayer, studying Scripture, attending worship, and serving others are all actions that we engage in regularly, but these repeated practices are not meaningless routines. They are instead instrumental in drawing us closer to God and aligning our hearts with His will.

God often leads us through repeated trials or tasks to help us develop specific virtues. James 1:2-4 (ESV) reminds us of this when it says, "Count it all joy, my brothers, when you meet trials of various kinds, for you know that the testing of your faith produces steadfastness. And let steadfastness have its full effect, that you may be perfect and complete, lacking in nothing." The concept of steadfastness here is the perseverance we gain through repetition. The repeated testing of our faith is designed to produce in us a mature and resilient character that is prepared for greater challenges.

Beyond perseverance, repetition serves to deepen our understanding and strengthen our habits. When we engage in regular biblical disciplines, we internalize God's truths and become more like Christ. Just as athletes train for an event by repeating certain exercises, we, too, grow spiritually through disciplined repetition. In Deuteronomy 6:6-7 (ESV), God instructs the Israelites, "And these words that I command you today shall be on your heart. You shall teach them diligently to your children, and shall talk of them when you sit in your house, and when you walk by the way, and when you lie down, and when you rise." This verse emphasizes the importance of continually revisiting and teaching God's Word, highlighting how repetition reinforces our faith and shapes our lives.

Finally, repetition teaches us patience and reliance on God. Sometimes, we go through seasons where we face the same challenges over and over. It can be frustrating, but these repeated experiences often serve to refine us, teaching us to depend more on God's strength and wisdom. In 2 Corinthians 12:9 (ESV), Paul writes, "But he said to me, 'My grace is sufficient for you, for my power is made perfect in weakness.'" Repeated trials humble us and remind us that our own strength is limited, leading us to rely more fully on God's grace.

In programming, repetition also plays a critical role. Often, we encounter problems that require us to repeat actions multiple times, whether we're processing a list of items or simulating ongoing game actions. Iteration structures like the while loop and the for loop allow us to perform these repeated actions efficiently and effectively. However, just as repetition in life requires intentionality and purpose, the design of our loops requires careful planning. Without a clear strategy, repetitive code can become inefficient, difficult to manage, or even produce unintended results.

In this chapter, we will explore how to use iteration structures to solve problems in Alex's game world, focusing on one of the most fundamental elements of game design: the game loop. This loop represents the heartbeat of the game, driving the ongoing process of turns, player actions, and interactions. We'll introduce a new problem-solving strategy called Repeating with Purpose, which emphasizes the importance of planning loops thoughtfully. This strategy involves identifying patterns, distinguishing between elements that remain constant and those that change with each iteration, and making deliberate decisions about how and when to iterate.

As Alex applies the five-step problem-solving process, he will learn how to leverage both `while` loops and `for` loops effectively. The `while` loop will power the main game loop, continuously prompting the player to take turns until they decide to stop. Meanwhile, the `for` loop will manage repeated actions within each turn, such as giving the player a set number of attempts to collect resources. By approaching repetition with intentionality, Alex can design loops that not only accomplish their tasks but also enhance the overall efficiency, clarity, and functionality of his game. Let's begin by understanding the problem Alex faces in implementing this game loop and how repetition will help bring his game world to life.

Step 1. Understand the Problem

In Alex's game, players take turns to interact with the game world, collecting resources, facing challenges, and working toward various goals. One of the key problems Alex faces is designing a game loop. A **game loop** is a structure that allows the player to repeatedly take actions until they decide to stop or reach a certain milestone. This game loop will drive the ongoing game play, continuously prompting the player to engage with the game world and track their progress.

A critical part of each turn in the game loop is the task of collecting resources. Since the game will encourage players to gather enough resources to earn rewards, Alex needs a way to repeat the resource-collecting process within each turn. Rather than requiring the player to manually input each action or repeatedly start the process over, Alex wants to automate the game loop so that it handles the repetitive nature of turns and resource collection efficiently.

To solve this problem, Alex needs to recognize that he's working with two types of repetition. The first is the main game loop, which repeats the player's turns until they decide to end the game. This loop will allow the player to collect resources, take actions, and interact with the game world repeatedly. The second is a more focused loop within each turn, where Alex wants to give the player multiple attempts to collect resources, providing a set number of chances to gather as many resources as possible during their turn.

These loops must be purpose-driven, continuing only as long as necessary. The game loop should repeat until the player decides to stop playing, while the resource-collection loop should run a specific number of times each turn. By understanding that the core problem involves both continuous repetition (the game loop) and controlled repetition (the resource attempts), Alex is ready to move to the next step: planning how to implement these loops to ensure that the game is engaging, efficient, and purposeful.

Step 2. Plan the Solution

Now that Alex understands that repetition is at the heart of the problem, it's time to plan how to solve it. This is where we introduce our next problem-solving strategy: Repeating with Purpose.

The key to solving repetition-based problems lies in defining the action that needs to be repeated, as well as when and how to stop. For Alex, this means thinking through the game loop that will govern his game's core functionality.

First, Alex considers the main action that will be repeated each turn: the process of running the game turn itself. Each turn includes allowing the player to collect resources, which requires its own sequence of actions. When setting up this loop, it's essential for Alex to identify repeating patterns in the problem. As Alex examines the task, he identifies which parts remain consistent and which elements vary. This allows him to structure his loops to carry out necessary actions while adapting to the unique requirements of each turn. For example, although the overall structure of each turn follows the same pattern, specific details, such as the number of resources collected, change with each iteration. By identifying these variations, Alex can determine what belongs inside the loop unchanged and what should be replaced with a variable that can update with each pass through the loop.

Next, Alex considers the stopping conditions for each loop. The game loop itself will continue if the player chooses to keep playing, which provides a natural end condition. Within each game turn, Alex plans to allow the player a set number of resource-collection attempts, such as three. This repetition should have a defined purpose, stopping after the player has had the maximum allowed attempts.

Finally, Alex needs to determine how to control these conditions effectively. The game loop will rely on player input to decide whether to continue or quit, while the resource-collection loop within each turn will automatically stop once the player has used all three attempts. This control structure enables Alex to align each loop's behavior with the player's progress and choices, ensuring that the game responds dynamically to the player's actions.

To better understand how these loops will work together, Text Box 4.1 outlines the main game loop with pseudo-code. This will help Alex think through how the game's flow will function.

Text Box 4.1: Game Loop & Resource Collection Pseudo-code

While the player wants to keep playing
    Display a message to start a new turn
    Set the total resources collected to zero for this turn
    Repeat the resource collection process the maximum number of attempts allowed
        Simulate collecting resources and update the total collected
        Display the amount collected in this attempt
    Display the total resources collected during the turn
    Ask the player if they want to play another turn
End the game when the player decides to stop

In this pseudo-code, the game starts by displaying a message to indicate the beginning of a new turn. The total resources collected for the turn is set to zero, allowing Alex to track how many resources the player collects during each turn. The main game loop is controlled by the condition that the player chooses to continue playing. Inside this loop, Alex plans for a separate repetitive process to represent the player's resource-collection attempts. This separate process runs three times, allowing the player to collect resources multiple times in each turn. At the end of each turn, the game displays the total resources collected, and the player is asked if they want to continue.

In addition to the pseudo-code, Alex can use an activity diagram to gain a visual perspective on the flow of the game loop and the resource-collection process. The activity diagram in Figure 4.1 illustrates how the main game loop begins with a diamond-shaped decision point that checks if the player wants to continue playing.

If the answer is no, the flow follows an arrow leading to a terminal node, which ends the game. If the player chooses to continue, the flow moves into the nested loop for resource collection, represented by three sequential passes. Within this nested loop, another decision point checks whether the player has remaining attempts. If they do, the flow loops back to collect more resources, tracking each attempt until the limit of three is reached. After completing the resource-collection loop, the game displays the total resources collected in that turn, and the flow returns to the beginning of the main game loop.

The activity diagram provides a structured view of the decision-making process, showing where the program branches based on player choices and attempt limits. By combining this visual model with the pseudo-code, Alex can ensure that the game loop and resource-collection logic are designed effectively, accommodating the player's interactions and tracking resources throughout the game. This dual approach helps Alex anticipate the program's flow, confirm the accuracy of his design, and prepare for efficient code implementation.

To effectively manage the game's flow, Alex expands his design by introducing a new Game class, which becomes the central hub of the game's architecture. This new class will oversee the player's actions

Figure 4.1: Activity Diagram

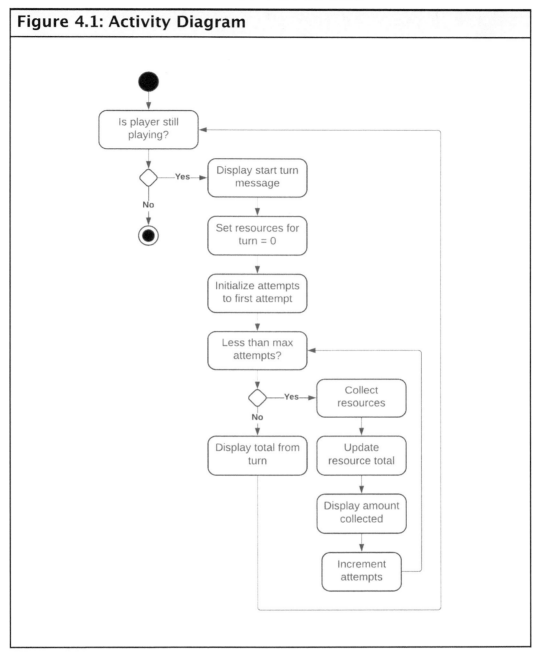

and control the main game play loop. To visualize these changes, Alex updates his class diagram, as shown in Figure 4.2. The updated diagram shows how the Game class connects with the Player class. This connection reflects how the game will handle both the player's actions and the overall flow.

Alex starts by adding a `Player` property to the `Game` class. This property will hold an instance of the `Player` class, giving the game control over the player's actions like collecting resources and tracking their score. This connection simplifies the game's logic, ensuring that player-related tasks remain the responsibility of the `Player` class but also within the control of the `Game` class.

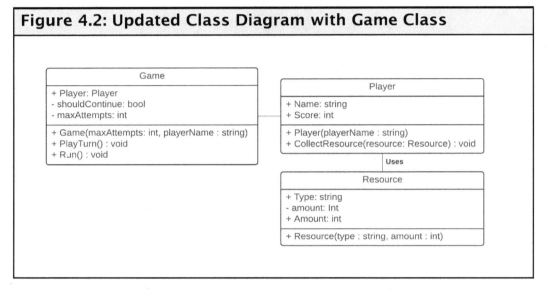

Figure 4.2: Updated Class Diagram with Game Class

To control the flow of the game, Alex also adds a private field named `shouldContinue` to the `Game` class, as indicated by the minus symbol (-) before the field name in the diagram. This field works as a simple flag, checking whether the player wants to keep playing or quit, allowing Alex to easily manage the loop's flow. By marking the field as private, Alex ensures the `Game` class is the only class that can see or change this field.

Next, Alex adds a private `maxAttempts` field to set the number of resource collection attempts allowed per turn. This field will allow Alex to adjust the number of allowed attempts in the future without needing to rewrite core parts of the game's logic.

To make sure the `Game` class is ready to manage the player right from the beginning, Alex adds a constructor. This constructor will take an initial value for the maximum number of attempts in each turn, as well as the player's name. By setting up the game's conditions at the start,

Alex makes it easier to tweak things like the number of attempts later, if needed.

Next, Alex adds a `PlayTurn` method to the `Game` class, which encapsulates the process of running a single turn in the game. Within this method, Alex can include the logic to allow the player to collect resources up to `maxAttempts` times, using a loop to repeat the resource collection process as needed. The `PlayTurn` method will leverage the `Player` property to directly access the player's `CollectResource` method, ensuring that resource collection is handled consistently and efficiently.

Finally, Alex adds a `Run` method to serve as the central point where the main game loop is controlled. By keeping the primary game loop inside the `Run` method, Alex keeps the game's high-level structure easy to follow and separates it from the details of individual turns. This will make the code easier to read and maintain. If Alex ever wants to adjust how the game ends or introduce new game play features, he can simply update the `Run` method without changing other parts of the game.

The updated class diagram serves as a road map for Alex, showing how each piece fits together and highlighting the role of the `Game` class in orchestrating the game play. By starting with this clear structure, Alex can approach the implementation phase with confidence, knowing that he's building on a solid foundation.

Step 3. Implement the Solution

With the design of the `Game` class in place it's time for Alex to implement the actual code. The `Game` class will act as the central hub for controlling the game's flow, including player actions and the overall game play loop.

At the core of this class is the `Player` property, which stores an instance of a `Player` class. Additionally, the `Game` class contains two private fields: `shouldContinue`, a Boolean flag, and `maxAttempts`, an integer. Code Block 4.1 shows Alex's initial implementation of the `Game` class. At this stage, Alex is still working through the details of the `PlayTurn` and `Run` methods, so he begins with method stubs for now. A **method stub** is an empty method declaration that serves as a placeholder. This approach allows Alex to build the class structure before filling in the specific logic for these methods.

Code Block 4.1: Initial Implementation of the Game Class

```
 1| public class Game
 2| {
 3|    // Properties and Fields
 4|
 5|    // Relationship property that stores the player
 6|    public Player Player { get; set; }
 7|
 8|    // Flag to determine if the game should continue
 9|    private bool shouldContinue;
10|
11|    // Number of resource collection attempts per turn
12|    private int maxAttempts;
13|
14|    // Constructor
15|    public Game(int maxAttempts, string playerName)
16|    {
17|       this.maxAttempts = maxAttempts;
18|       shouldContinue = true;
19|
20|       // Instantiate the Player object
21|       Player = new(playerName);
22|    }
23|
24|    // Method to handle resource collection for a single turn
25|    public void PlayTurn()
26|    {
27|       // TODO: Add logic for playing a turn
28|    }
29|
30|    // Main game loop method
31|    public void Run()
32|    {
33|       // TODO: Add logic for running the game loop
34|    }
35| }
```

To tie everything together, Alex creates a constructor for the Game class, which sets up the initial state of the game. Inside the constructor, Alex assigns the maxAttempts parameter to the private maxAttempts field, and sets shouldContinue to true, ensuring that the game is ready to run. Additionally, the Player property is instantiated by creating a new Player object, passing in the player's name.

The this Keyword

You might notice the use of the this keyword in line 17 in Code Block 4.1. The this keyword is used to distinguish between the parameter maxAttempts and the field maxAttempts within the class.

In object-oriented programming, it's possible for the names of parameters passed to a constructor (or method) to "shadow" or hide the names of fields within the class. In this case, both the parameter and the class field are named maxAttempts. Without the this keyword, the constructor would assume that both maxAttempts refer to the parameter, leaving no way to assign the value to the class's field.

The this keyword clarifies that we are referring to the field that belongs to the current instance of the Game class, not the constructor parameter. It tells the program, "Use the maxAttempts field that belongs to *this* instance of the class and assign it the value of the parameter maxAttempts."

Notice that we don't need the this keyword for the shouldContinue field or for the Player property. In those cases, the constructor doesn't have a parameter named shouldContinue, nor does it have a parameter named Player, so there's no conflict between the field names and the parameter names. When no shadowing occurs, the field or property name can be used directly, without the need for this.

The While Loop

Before getting into Alex's design for the Run method, let's first introduce the while loop, one of the most fundamental iteration structures in programming. A **while loop** allows a block of code to repeat as long as a specified condition remains true. It's commonly used in situations where you don't know exactly how many times the loop needs to run, but you know the condition that determines when the loop should stop. The basic structure of a while loop is shown in Code Block 4.2.

The loop evaluates the condition at the start of each iteration. If the condition evaluates to true, the code inside the curly braces runs. After executing the code block, the loop checks the condition again, and the process repeats. If the condition is false, the loop stops, and the program moves on to the next section of code.

Code Block 4.2: The While Loop Structure

```
1| while (condition)
2| {
3|    // Code to be executed repeatedly
4| }
```

This structure is particularly useful in situations where the number of repetitions depends on user input, changing values, or dynamic conditions within the game. In Alex's case, the while loop will drive the main game loop within the Run method, continuing to play turns only if the player wants to keep playing.

Let's move on to how Alex implements the while loop in the Run method. The Run method will be responsible for handling the main game loop and determining when the player wants to quit, so Alex designs the while loop to continue running if the player wants to keep playing, which is controlled by the shouldContinue flag. After each turn, the game will prompt the player to decide whether they want to continue. If the player enters anything other than "y," the loop will terminate, and the game will end. Code Block 4.3 shows how Alex implements the Run method.

Code Block 4.3: Implementation of the Run Method

```
1| public void Run()
2| {
3|    while (shouldContinue)
4|    {
5|       Console.WriteLine("Starting a new turn...");
6|
7|       // Call the method to handle a single turn
8|       PlayTurn();
9|
10|       // Ask the player if they want to continue playing
11|       Console.Write("Want to play another turn (y/n)? ");
12|       string input = Console.ReadLine();
13|
14|       // Update the flag based on the player's input
15|       if (input.ToLower() != "y")
16|       {
17|          shouldContinue = false;
18|          Console.WriteLine("Thank you for playing!");
19|       }
20|    }
21| }
```

In this method, the while loop checks the value of the `shouldContinue` field, and if it is `true`, then the game loop can officially begin. Before the player plays their turn, the loop prints a message to signal the start of each new turn. The loop then calls the `PlayTurn` method, which will handle the specifics of what happens during a single turn. After the turn is completed, the game asks the player if they want to continue. If the player enters "y," the loop will run again for another turn. Otherwise, the `shouldContinue` flag is set to false, ending the loop and stopping the game.

The For Loop

Before we get into the details of Alex's design for the `PlayTurn` method, let's first introduce the `for` loop, another important iteration structure in programming. While the `while` loop is useful when we don't know in advance how many times the loop needs to run, the **for loop** is ideal when we do know the exact number of iterations required. The basic structure of a for loop is shown in Code Block 4.4.

Code Block 4.4: The For Loop Structure

```
for (initialization; condition; update)
{
    // Code to be executed repeatedly
}
```

The for loop operates in three key stages. First, there's the initialization phase, which occurs once at the start of the loop. This is where a counter variable is typically initialized to set the starting point, like setting `int i = 0`. Next, the loop evaluates the condition before each iteration. As long as this condition is true, the loop will continue running. However, once the condition becomes false, the loop stops, preventing further iterations. Finally, after each iteration, the update step takes place, where the counter variable is modified, often incremented by 1 (e.g., `i++`). This update ensures the loop progresses and eventually meets the condition for stopping.

For example, a loop designed to run 10 times would look like the code shown in Code Block 4.5. In this case, the loop starts by setting `i` to 0. It continues running as long as i is less than 10, and after each iteration, i is incremented by 1.

Code Block 4.5: A For Loop Example

```
1| for (int i = 0; i < 10; i++)
2| {
3|     // Code to execute 10 times
4| }
```

The for loop is ideal for situations where we have a fixed number of actions that need to be performed. In Alex's game, each turn will allow the player to collect resources a specific number of times, making the for loop a perfect fit for the PlayTurn method. By using a for loop, Alex can ensure that the player gets exactly maxAttempts opportunities to gather resources. Code Block 4.6 shows how Alex implements the PlayTurn method.

Code Block 4.6: The PlayTurn Method

```
1| public void PlayTurn()
2| {
3|     int turnTotal = 0;
4|     for (int i = 0; i < maxAttempts; i++)
5|     {
6|         Console.Write($"Attempt {i + 1}/{maxAttempts}: ");
7|         Console.Write("Enter number of resources collected: ");
8|         int attemptTotal = int.Parse(Console.ReadLine());
9|         turnTotal += attemptTotal;
10|     }
11|     // Collect resources and add to the player's total
12|     Resource resource = new("Wood", turnTotal);
13|     Player.CollectResource(resource);
14|     Console.WriteLine($"Collected this turn: {turnTotal}");
15| }
```

In the PlayTurn method, the for loop runs maxAttempts number of iterations, giving the player multiple chances to collect resources in a single turn. For each attempt, the game displays their attempt number out of the maximum possible attempts. It then prompts the player to enter the number of resources they've collected, which is then added to the running total for the turn. Once the loop finishes, the total resources collected during the turn are displayed, providing feedback to the player about their progress.

By starting with the overall Game class, then building the Run method, and finally building the PlayTurn method, Alex ensures that each part of his code is built on a solid foundation. This top-down approach to design allows Alex to focus first on the larger structure of the game before drilling down into the details of each turn. With the Game class complete, Alex has established the core game play mechanics, and he's now ready to test the game and ensure that everything runs correctly.

Step 4. Test the Solution

To test the solution effectively, Alex needs to focus on both the individual components and the overall game play experience. In this case, Alex's game includes two key loops: the main game loop in the Run method and the resource collection loop in the PlayTurn method. Each of these loops must be tested to ensure they function correctly and interact with each other seamlessly.

Test Case 1: Basic Game Flow

The first test should ensure that the game runs correctly from start to finish. Alex begins by simulating a complete game play session to see how the game responds to different inputs. This includes making sure that the game prompts the player to collect resources, updates the total resource count, and checks whether the player wants to continue or exit the game.

Alex begins the test case with the code in Code Block 4.7. In this test, Alex sets the maximum number of attempts per turn to three and uses his name as the player's name.

Code Block 4.7: Test Case 1 Code

```
1| // Instantiate the Game class
2| Game myGame = new(3, "Alex");
3|
4| // Start the game by calling the Run method
5| myGame.Run();
```

Alex simulates a few turns where the player enters different amounts of resources collected. He checks that the game correctly asks if the player wants to continue and that the game responds correctly when the player chooses to continue and when the player chooses to quit. Text Box 4.2 shows the output from this test case.

Text Box 4.2: Test Case 1 Output

```
Starting a new turn...
Attempt 1/3: Enter number of resources collected: 10
Attempt 2/3: Enter number of resources collected: 15
Attempt 3/3: Enter number of resources collected: 20
Keep going to reach your goal.
Collected this turn: 45
Want to play another turn (y/n)? y
Starting a new turn...
Attempt 1/3: Enter number of resources collected: 30
Attempt 2/3: Enter number of resources collected: 25
Attempt 3/3: Enter number of resources collected: 10
Good job! You're halfway there.
Collected this turn: 65
Want to play another turn (y/n)? n
Thank you for playing!
```

Test Case 2: Resource Collection Logic

The next test focuses on the resource collection process during a single turn. Alex wants to ensure that the player can input different amounts of resources during each attempt and that the game correctly adds these values to the total resources for the turn. In this test, Alex simulates a scenario where the player collects varying amounts of resources, such as 100, 51, and 0. He then checks that the game accurately calculates and displays the total for that turn. Text Box 4.3 shows the output from this test case.

Text Box 4.3: Test Case 2 Output

```
Starting a new turn...
Attempt 1/3: Enter number of resources collected: 100
Attempt 2/3: Enter number of resources collected: 51
Attempt 3/3: Enter number of resources collected: 0
You earned a score bonus!
Collected this turn: 151
Want to play another turn (y/n)? n
Thank you for playing!
```

Testing Edge Cases

Alex should also test some edge cases to make sure the game handles unexpected inputs appropriately. For example, he could test what happens if the player enters a negative number of resources or inputs an unusually large number. It's also important to test whether the game responds correctly if the player presses "enter" without entering a value. Text Box 4.4 shows the output from one of Alex's tests, where he pressed "enter" without entering a value.

Text Box 4.4: Test Case 3 Output

Starting a new turn...
Attempt 1/3: Enter number of resources collected:
Unhandled exception. System.FormatException: The input string '' was not in a correct format.
  at System.Number.ThrowOverflowOrFormatException(ParsingStatus status, ReadOnlySpan`1 value, TypeCode type)
  at System.Int32.Parse(String s)
  at ProblemSolving.Game.PlayTurn() in ...Game.cs:line 47
  at ProblemSolving.Game.Run() in ...Game.cs:line 24
  at Program.<Main>$(String[] args) in ...Program.cs:line 7

To his surprise, he discovered a bug that caused his program to crash! To fix this bug, Alex can modify his code to handle invalid input more gracefully. One effective way to do this is by using a while loop with the int.TryParse() method. The int.TryParse() method attempts to convert the user's input into an integer and returns true if the conversion is successful, or false if the input is invalid. This allows Alex to repeatedly prompt the player until they enter a valid number. Code Block 4.8 shows Alex's revised code for the PlayTurn method.

In this updated code (lines 8 through 20), Alex uses a while loop to repeatedly prompt the player for input until they provide a valid number. If int.TryParse() successfully converts the player's input to an integer, the while loop ends, and the game continues. If the input is invalid (such as when the player presses "enter" without typing a number), the game displays an error message and asks the player to try again. This approach ensures the program handles input errors gracefully and doesn't crash.

In the updated code, you'll notice the use of the out keyword in the int.TryParse() method (line 15). The out keyword is used when a method needs to return multiple values. In the case of int.TryParse(), the method returns a bool (indicating whether the conversion was successful), but it also "outputs" the converted value into the variable specified after the out keyword (in this case, the collected variable).

Code Block 4.8: Revised PlayTurn Method

```
1  public void PlayTurn()
2  {
3     int turnTotal = 0;
4     for (int i = 0; i < maxAttempts; i++)
5     {
6        int attemptTotal = 0;
7        bool isValidInput = false;
8        while (!isValidInput)
9        {
10          Console.Write($"Attempt {i + 1}/{maxAttempts}: ");
11          Console.Write("Enter number of resources collected: ");
12          string input = Console.ReadLine();
13
14          // Try to parse the input
15          isValidInput = int.TryParse(input, out attemptTotal);
16          if (!isValidInput)
17          {
18             Console.WriteLine("Invalid input. Please try again.");
19          }
20       }
21       turnTotal += attemptTotal;
22     }
23     // Collect resources and add to the player's total
24     Resource resource = new("Wood", turnTotal);
25     Player.CollectResource(resource);
26     Console.WriteLine($"Collected this turn: {turnTotal}");
27  }
```

When the player enters a valid number, int.TryParse() attempts to convert the input string into an integer. If it succeeds, the method stores the resulting integer value in attemptTotal, and the program proceeds. If the input isn't valid (e.g., the player enters letters or presses "enter" without providing a value), int.TryParse() returns false, and the attemptTotal variable remains unchanged.

Running through these test cases enabled Alex to spot and resolve the issues with his code. Fixing problems like handling invalid inputs helps make the game more reliable and enjoyable for players no matter what they type in. Alex is now ready to consider ways to optimize his solution.

Step 5. Refine and Optimize

With the game now functioning as expected, Alex has successfully tackled the core problem of looping through game turns and collecting resources. However, there's always room for improvement. Now that the initial version of the Game class is working, it's time to look for ways to streamline the code, make it more efficient, and even simplify the structure where possible.

One simple but meaningful improvement is to add feedback at the end of each turn to show the player their current score. This can be done by adding a Console.WriteLine statement at the end of the PlayTurn method. Code Block 4.9 shows how the PlayTurn method can be modified to include this feedback. By displaying the player's current score at the end of each turn, Alex adds a small but valuable piece of feedback to keep the player engaged and informed about their progress.

Code Block 4.9: Refined PlayTurn Method

```
 1  public void PlayTurn()
 2  {
 3    int turnTotal = 0;
 4    for (int i = 0; i < maxAttempts; i++)
 5    {
 6      int attemptTotal = 0;
 7      bool isValidInput = false;
 8      while (!isValidInput)
 9      {
10        Console.Write($"Attempt {i + 1}/{maxAttempts}: ");
11        Console.Write("Enter number of resources collected: ");
12        string input = Console.ReadLine();
13        // Try to parse the input
14        isValidInput = int.TryParse(input, out attemptTotal);
15        if (!isValidInput)
16        {
17          Console.WriteLine("Invalid input. Please try again.");
18        }
19      }
20      turnTotal += attemptTotal;
21    }
22    // Collect resources and add to the player's total
23    Resource resource = new("Wood", turnTotal);
24    Player.CollectResource(resource);
25    Console.WriteLine($"Collected this turn: {turnTotal}");
26    Console.WriteLine($"Your score: {Player.Score}");
27  }
```

The do..while Loop

In the initial implementation of Alex's game, the main game loop in the Run method was structured using a while loop. A more fitting choice for the flow of the game would be the **do..while loop**. This type of loop better aligns with how the game should operate.

The key distinction between a while loop and a do..while loop lies in when the condition is checked. In a do..while loop, the code inside the loop runs at least once before the condition is evaluated. This behavior makes perfect sense for Alex's game. Code Block 4.10 shows how Alex updates the Run method to use a do..while loop.

For the overall game loop, the game should always run at least one full turn before asking the player whether they want to continue. This ensures that the player has a chance to experience the game before deciding to quit. While the change that Alex made to the Run method doesn't change the way the game functions, it does make the purpose of the game loop clearer.

Code Block 4.10: Optimized Run Method

```
 1| public void Run()
 2| {
 3|   do
 4|   {
 5|     Console.WriteLine("Starting a new turn...");
 6|
 7|     // Call the method to handle a single turn
 8|     PlayTurn();
 9|
10|     // Ask the player if they want to continue playing
11|     Console.Write("Want to play another turn (y/n)? ");
12|     string input = Console.ReadLine();
13|
14|     // Update the flag based on the player's input
15|     if (input.ToLower() != "y")
16|     {
17|       shouldContinue = false;
18|       Console.WriteLine("Thank you for playing!");
19|     }
20|   } while (shouldContinue);
21| }
```

Recap: Repeat with Purpose

As Alex worked through his solution, he used the problem-solving strategy of Repeating with Purpose to guide his design of the game's loops. This strategy emphasizes the intentionality behind repetition, ensuring that each loop has a clear purpose and stops when the goal is reached. By focusing on the parts of the game's logic that remained consistent (commonality) and which parts changed (variability), Alex was able to create loops that efficiently handle repeated tasks while maintaining flexibility for changing inputs. By Repeating with Purpose, Alex made sure the loops were not only functional but also optimized to handle the flow of the game in a way that made the code clearer and more efficient. Let's add Repeating with Purpose to your growing problem-solving toolkit in Text Box 4.5.

Text Box 4.5: Problem–Solving Strategies

1. **Follow the Five-Step Problem-Solving Process**
   Understand the problem, plan the solution, implement the solution, test the solution, and finally refine and optimize it. This structured approach will help you systematically tackle any programming challenge you encounter.

2. **Break Down Big Problems into Smaller Parts**
   Whenever you face a large, complicated problem, break it down into smaller, simpler parts. In programming, this often involves using objects and classes to represent different pieces of the problem. By focusing on one piece at a time, you'll find the overall solution much easier to achieve.

3. **Evaluate Multiple Scenarios**
   Plan for different conditions and map out the appropriate actions for each. This includes identifying the extreme values at the edges of the expected inputs and testing how the program behaves under these conditions.

4. **Repeating with Purpose**
   When designing loops, analyze the tasks to be repeated, identifying what stays consistent (commonality) and what changes (variability) in each iteration. Be intentional about how and why you're repeating actions, and ensure that loops serve a clear purpose, stopping when the goal is achieved.

Summary

In this chapter, we explored how repetition plays a crucial role in both spiritual growth and programming. Just as God uses repeated experiences to refine our character and faith, repetition in programming requires intentionality and purpose to produce effective and efficient solutions. Through Alex's game design, we introduced the concept of Repeating with Purpose, emphasizing the importance of planning loops thoughtfully, identifying patterns of commonality and variability, and ensuring that each loop serves a clear and defined purpose.

Alex's challenge in this chapter was to create a game loop that allowed the player to take turns collecting resources while managing how often these actions were repeated. By using a while loop for the game's core game play and a for loop to control the number of attempts within each turn, Alex ensured that his game responded correctly to the player's actions.

We also introduced key iteration structures like the while and for loops, which allow code to repeat actions efficiently. Alex refined and optimized his solution by switching from while loops to do..while loops in certain cases, ensuring the game's code clearly communicated the game's purpose. Finally, we discussed testing strategies and introduced ways to handle potential bugs, such as using input validation with int.TryParse() to make the game more robust and reliable.

Review Questions

1. How does repetition play a role in both Christian spiritual growth and programming? Provide examples from each context.

2. In what situations outside of gaming might you need to repeat actions in a program? Describe how you would use a loop to handle one of these situations.

3. Explain how the strategy of Repeating with Purpose helps in planning loops in a program. Why is it important to identify both the common actions and the actions that change with each repetition?

4. When would you use a while loop instead of a for loop? Think of everyday tasks where each type of loop would work well.

5. Consider a situation where a person needs to log daily activities, such as the number of hours they study each day. How would you use a loop to repeat the process of asking for and recording their input for a whole week?

6. When asking for user input (like a person's age), why is it important to check that the input is valid? How can a loop help with this task?

7. In what situations would it be helpful to use a do..while loop instead of a while loop? Think of a situation in everyday life where you'd always need to complete at least one action before deciding whether to repeat it.

8. How does using `int.TryParse()` or similar methods make your program more user-friendly?

9. In what situations is it helpful to have a flag variable (like `shouldContinue`) to control whether your program keeps running?

10. When designing a program that repeats actions, why should you test for edge cases (like entering a negative number or not entering anything)? How can this help make sure your program works well for all users?

Practice Problems

1. **Collecting Daily Sales Data**. Write a program that asks a store manager to input the total sales for each day of the week (7 days). Use a loop to ask for the sales and calculate the total sales at the end of the week. After collecting the data, display the total sales and the average sales per day.

2. **Quiz Score Entry**. Create a program that allows a teacher to enter the quiz scores for a group of students. The program should continue to ask for scores until the user inputs a negative number to stop. If a score is invalid (e.g., above 100), the program should print an error message and ask for the score again. At the end, display the average score for the class.

3. **Movie Rating**. Write a program that asks users to enter their rating for a movie (from 1 to 5). The program should always ask for the user's rating at least once and continue asking until they enter a valid rating. After the user inputs a valid rating, display a thank-you message.

4. **Inventory Restocking**. A small shop owner needs to restock a list of 5 items. Write a program that asks the owner how much of each item they want to add to inventory, referring to each item with the numbers 1 through 5. Use a for loop to repeat the process for the 5 items, and then display the total quantity of the items restocked.

5. **Temperature Logger**. Write a program that prompts the user for temperature data from a weather station. The user should be prompted 10 times to input a temperature for a different day, referring to each temperature with the numbers 1 through 10. If they enter an invalid temperature (e.g., below -50°C or above 50°C), the program should display an error and repeatedly ask for the temperature until a valid temperature is provided. Once all valid temperatures are entered, the program should display the highest and lowest temperatures recorded.

6. **Gym Workout Tracker**. Create a program that tracks a user's workout. The user should enter the number of reps they completed for each of 5 exercises. Use a for loop to repeat the input process for the 5 exercises, referring to each exercise with the numbers 1 through 5. After all exercises are entered, display the total number of reps completed for all exercises for the entire workout.

7. **Parking Lot System**. You are designing a system for a parking lot where the capacity is 50 cars. Write a program that asks how many cars have entered the parking lot today and updates the total. If the input value is more than 50 or a negative number, the program should display an error and ask for the input again. Use a loop to handle this. At the end, display the number of spots remaining in the parking lot.

8. **Bank Account Manager**. Create a program that simulates basic bank account management. The user should be able to choose from the following actions: deposit, withdraw, check balance, or quit. Use a do..while loop to repeat these actions until the user decides to quit. Include input validation to ensure that the user cannot withdraw

more money than they have in the account, and that deposit and withdrawal amounts are positive.

"As you do not know the way the spirit comes to the bones in the womb of a woman with child, so you do not know the work of God who makes everything."
Ecclesiastes 11:5 (ESV)

CHAPTER 5

SCOPE, RANDOMNESS, AND ENUMERATIONS

Introduction

The Bible provides many principles that guide how we interact with others, how we manage the resources God entrusts to our care, and how we respond to the unpredictable nature of the world around us. One of these principles is the importance of boundaries. God's Word reminds us that we must guard our hearts and set healthy limits in our relationships. Proverbs 4:23 (ESV) instructs us, "Keep your heart with all vigilance, for from it flow the springs of life." This passage reminds us to be intentional with the boundaries we set, so that we guard our hearts from worldy influences.

The Bible also teaches us that nothing we have is truly our own. Psalm 24:1 (ESV) says, "The earth is the Lord's and the fullness thereof, the world and those who dwell therein." Everything we possess, our talents, resources, and even the time we spend coding, is a gift from God. We are merely stewards, called to manage these gifts wisely. In Luke 16:10 (ESV), Jesus reminded his disciples that "One who is faithful in a very little is also faithful in much." God calls us to manage well the resources

He entrusts to our care, whether small or large. This applies not only to physical resources but also to the way we manage our responsibilities and relationships.

While setting purposeful boundaries and proper planning for the use of entrusted resources are important, we often face situations that we cannot predict or control. In these moments, the Bible reminds us to trust in God's sovereignty and wisdom. Ecclesiastes 11:5 (ESV) tells us, "As you do not know the way the spirit comes to the bones in the womb of a woman with child, so you do not know the work of God who makes everything." This passage reminds us that while life can feel random or unpredictable, God is ultimately in control of all things.

From the very beginning, God has brought order out of chaos. In the opening chapter of Genesis, we see God speak the world into existence and bring form and structure to what was formless. He separated light from darkness, waters from dry land, and established the rhythms of life. Throughout Scripture, we are reminded that God is a God of order, not confusion (1 Corinthians 14:33). His wisdom gives us structure and clarity, allowing us to live purposefully.

In programming, the principles of stewardship, setting boundaries, and trusting in God's wisdom are reflected in how we manage code structure and resources. In this chapter, Alex will apply these biblical principles to introduce key programming concepts: managing variable scope and lifetime, introducing randomness to the game's resource collection, and using enumerations to bring order to the types of resources. Much like the boundaries, stewardship, and trust that we are called to exercise in our lives, these concepts help us structure our programs in a way that ensures efficiency, clarity, and intentionality.

Step 1. Understand the Problem

As Alex continues developing his game, he realizes that adding an element of randomness will make the game play more engaging. Right now, the game is too predictable. Players currently specify the number of resources they collect during each turn, making the experience repetitive. Alex wants to introduce variety into the game, such as randomizing the number of resources a player collects on each turn. This randomness will add unpredictability, keeping players more engaged and offering new challenges and experiences each time they play.

However, this new feature brings up a few challenges. First, Alex needs to figure out how to generate random numbers in his code. This will allow him to vary the number of resources collected each turn. But randomness isn't always easy to manage. Alex needs to ensure that the random numbers generated behave as expected, without repeating patterns or predictable outcomes.

Second, introducing randomness also touches on the ideas of scope and lifetime. **Scope** is the concept that determines where different parts of the program can access and use certain variables, while **lifetime** defines how long the variable exists in memory. Alex will need to use a random number generator to create random numbers throughout the game, but he will need to ensure that it is shared across the game and properly controlled to make the randomization work correctly.

In addition to randomizing resource collection, Alex notices another area of the game that could be improved. Currently, the different types of resources that players collect, like wood or stone, are represented as string values. However, this approach feels unstructured, and it opens the possibility of typos or inconsistencies when referring to resource types in different parts of the code. For example, what if one part of the code spells "stone" as "Stone," while another part spells it as "stone" with a lowercase "s"? Such inconsistencies could lead to hard-to-find bugs.

Instead of using strings, which are prone to human error, Alex wants each resource type to be clearly defined in advance to avoid typos and misuse. This leads Alex to consider using **enumerations**, a tool in programming that allows you to define a set of related values under one category. By using an enumeration to represent resource types, Alex can ensure that the game only uses valid resource types without the possibility of typos.

With randomness adding excitement to the game play and enumerations helping to organize the different types of resources, Alex is now ready to move on to planning his solution.

Step 2. Plan the Solution

Planning a solution that introduces randomness while maintaining good control over the game's resource types requires two major changes to the game: implementing randomness for resource collection and organizing the types of resources using enumerations.

The Random Class

The first part of Alex's plan involves adding an element of unpredictability to the resource collection process. Instead of asking the player to manually enter the number of resources collected, Alex wants the game to assign a random number of resources on each turn. This randomness will vary the game play experience and keep it fresh.

To accomplish this, Alex plans to use the Random class, which is part of the System namespace. As its name implies, the Random class generates random numbers, but the way it does so is an important consideration. Unlike the intuitive idea of randomness that we might have as humans (such as drawing numbers from a hat), computers use mathematical functions to generate pseudo-random numbers based on an initial seed value. This means that if Alex creates multiple instances of the Random class too quickly, the game could produce predictable, repeated patterns. This happens because, by default, Random objects are seeded based on the current system time. If Alex creates several Random objects at nearly the same time, they might all receive similar seed values, causing them to generate a similar sequence of numbers.

To avoid this issue, Alex needs to ensure that only one instance of the Random class is used throughout the entire game. He can do this by making the Random object a static field in the Game class.

Additionally, Alex plans to limit the random number of resources collected so that they fall within a reasonable range. However, he needs to carefully consider the range of possible random values. If the range is too low, the player may never collect enough resources to earn a score bonus. On the other hand, if the range is too high, the game could become unbalanced, with players reaching their goals too quickly and losing interest.

After some thought, Alex settles on giving players a random number of resources between 20 and 50 each time they collect resources. This range is balanced enough to provide a realistic chance of surpassing the 100-resource threshold within a few attempts, making the score bonus both achievable and rewarding. Additionally, it keeps the variability manageable, ensuring that each collection is meaningful but doesn't overwhelm the player with an excessive number of resources. To generate this random range, Alex plans to use the `Next()` method from the `Random` class.

Enumerations

The second part of the solution involves replacing the loose string representation of resources with a more structured system. Right now, resource types like "wood" or "stone" are stored as plain strings, which can easily lead to mistakes. If Alex or another developer accidentally types "Wood" in one place and "wood" in another, the game's logic could fail to recognize that they refer to the same resource.

To solve this, Alex plans to introduce an enumeration (`enum`) to represent the different kinds of resources in the game. For instance, Alex can define an enumeration that includes specific kinds of resources such as wood, stone, graphite, and clay. This enumeration becomes a new variable type that Alex can use in place of `string` for the `Type` property in the `Resource` class.

Managing Variable Scope and Lifetime

Since the game involves multiple objects interacting with each other, Alex must carefully plan how to manage both the scope and lifetime of variables. As mentioned earlier, scope determines which parts of the program can access a variable, while lifetime defines how long the variable exists in memory. Together, these concepts ensure that the right boundaries are placed around each variable, so that variables are only available where and when appropriate to avoid unwanted behavior.

In Alex's case, the random object will need to have class-level visibility within the Game class and a lifetime that persists throughout the entire game. A static variable ensures that the Random object is created once and shared across all turns, so that the randomization logic doesn't result in predictable patterns. Additionally, by marking the random object as private, Alex limits its scope to the Game class, ensuring that only the Game class can access it. This boundary prevents other parts of the code from directly manipulating or interfering with the random number generator. In contrast, the enum for resource types will be public, as it's necessary for other parts of the program (like the Player class) to know about and use the different resource types.

Step 3. Implement the Solution

Now that Alex has a solid plan in place for managing randomness, variable scope, and resource types, it's time to implement the solution in code. The first task is to set up the Random object, ensuring it is used consistently throughout the game to generate unpredictable, yet structured outcomes for each resource collection. Alex will also introduce enumerations to make the resource types more readable and easier to manage.

Defining the Static Random Object

To implement the random number generation, Alex creates a static Random object in the Game class. As discussed earlier, the random object must be created only once to ensure a consistent stream of unpredictable numbers throughout the game. By marking the random object as static, Alex guarantees that it will persist throughout the lifetime of the game. Additionally, by declaring the random object as private, its scope is restricted to the Game class, preventing external interference. Code Block 5.1 shows how Alex sets up the Random object in the Game class.

Code Block 5.1: The Random Object

```
1  public class Game
2  {
3    private static Random random = new();
4    private bool shouldContinue;
5    private int maxAttempts;
6    public Player Player { get; set; }
7
8    public Game(int maxAttempts, string playerName)
9    {
10     this.maxAttempts = maxAttempts;
11     shouldContinue = true;
12     Player = new Player(playerName);
13   }
14
15   // Other methods here...
16 }
```

In the updated Game class, the Random object is declared and instantiated simultaneously. This means the random number generator is created even before the constructor of the class is executed, so the constructor doesn't need to instantiate it. By doing this, Alex ensures that the random number generator is available immediately.

Alex also declares random as a field rather than a property. While both fields and properties are scoped to the class, the choice to use a field here simplifies the code by avoiding the overhead of getter and setter accessors, which aren't necessary for a random number generator.

Enumerations

Next, Alex creates the ResourceType enumeration. This makes the resource types more maintainable and readable. This change means that ResourceType becomes a valid C# variable type, allowing Alex to use it anywhere a variable type is needed throughout the program. Code Block 5.2 shows the new enumeration for ResourceType.

Code Block 5.2: ResourceType Enumeration

```
1  public enum ResourceType
2  {
3    Wood, Stone, Steel, Graphite
4  }
```

As shown in Code Block 5.3, Alex next updates the Resource class to use the ResourceType enumeration for the Type property. He makes this update by changing the variable type of the Type property from string to ResourceType (line 3). Of course, Alex must also change the constructor parameter to match the enum type (line 7).

Code Block 5.3: Updated Resource Class

```
 1| public class Resource
 2| {
 3|     public ResourceType Type { get; set; }
 4|     private int amount;
 5|     public int Amount { ... }
 6|
 7|     public Resource(ResourceType type, int amount)
 8|     {
 9|         Type = type;
10|         Amount = amount;
11|     }
12| }
```

By updating the Resource class in this way, Alex has created a structured system that ensures resource types are standardized and easier to work with throughout the game.

Randomizing Resource Collection in the Game

As shown in Code Block 5.4, Alex updates the logic in the PlayTurn method to generate a random number of resources for each attempt (line 6). To give the player a reasonable chance of exceeding the 100-resource threshold and earning a score bonus, Alex uses the random object's Next() method with a range of 20 to 50 for each attempt.

The Next() method is called with two parameters: the minimum, *inclusive* bound and the *exclusive*, upper bound. Since Alex wants the player to collect between 20 and 50 resources, he used Next(20, 51), because 20 is included and 51 is excluded from that range.

Alex uses the new ResourceType.Wood enumeration value for all collection attempts (line 12). Although his code assumes the player is collecting wood for now, Alex can easily extend it to include other resource types in the future.

Code Block 5.4: Updated PlayTurn Method

```
 1| public void PlayTurn()
 2| {
 3|   int turnTotal = 0;
 4|   for (int i = 0; i < maxAttempts; i++)
 5|   {
 6|     int attemptTotal = random.Next(20, 51);
 7|     turnTotal += attemptTotal;
 8|     Console.Write($"Attempt {i + 1}/{maxAttempts}: ");
 9|     Console.WriteLine($"{attemptTotal} resources.");
10|   }
11|   // Collect resource and add to the player's total
12|   Resource resource = new(ResourceType.Wood, turnTotal);
13|   Player.CollectResource(resource);
14|   Console.WriteLine($"Collected this turn: {turnTotal}");
15|   Console.WriteLine($"Your score: {Player.Score}");
16| }
```

Step 4. Test the Solution

Now that Alex has implemented the solution, it's time to thoroughly test the new features. The first part of testing will involve simulating thousands of calls to the PlayTurn method to evaluate the randomness and ensure that the game mechanics work as intended. Specifically, Alex wants to determine how often the player's score increases after each turn and assess whether the randomness aligns with his game play goals.

In addition to testing the randomness, Alex also needs to verify that the new enumeration type for resource collection is working as expected. He will ensure that resource types are correctly assigned and referenced in the game logic, eliminating the possibility of errors caused by misspelled resource types. Together, these tests will confirm that the game operates correctly.

Test Case 1: Simulating Resource Collection

To ensure the random number generation behaves as expected, Alex decides to run a large-scale simulation of the resource collection process. By simulating thousands of calls to the PlayTurn method, Alex can gather enough data to evaluate how often players exceed the 100-resource threshold and earn a score bonus. This simulation will give Alex a clearer picture of whether the randomness provides the desired balance in game play, helping him determine if the resource collection system is fair and engaging. Code Block 5.5 shows the code Alex uses to run these simulations.

The test code uses a for loop to simulate many turns (10,000) by repeatedly calling the PlayTurn method. After each simulated turn, it checks whether the player's score increased (line 17), which indicates that the player collected over 100 resources in that turn.

Code Block 5.5: Simulation of Resource Collection

```
1| // Set up the game parameters
2| int sims = 10000;
3| // Number of resource collection attempts per turn
4| int maxAttempts = 3;
5| // To track how many times the player's score increases
6| int increases = 0;
7| // Instantiate Game with maxAttempts and a sample player name
8| Game game = new(maxAttempts, "TestPlayer");
9| // Run the simulation
10| for (int i = 0; i < sims; i++)
11| {
12|   // Store the player's score before the turn
13|   int initialScore = game.Player.Score;
14|   // Simulate a turn
15|   game.PlayTurn();
16|   // Check if the player's score increased after this turn
17|   if (game.Player.Score > initialScore)
18|   {
19|     increases++;
20|   }
21| }
22| // Display percentage of turns player's score increased
23| double increasePercent = (double)increases / sims * 100.0;
24| Console.WriteLine($"After {sims} simulations:");
25| Console.WriteLine($"The score increased {increases} times.");
26| Console.WriteLine($"This is {increasePercent}% of the turns.");
```

The code then calculates the percentage of turns that resulted in a score increase. Since percentages involve fractional numbers, the code casts the count of increases to double when calculating the percentage (line 23). This **type casting** ensures that the division operation results in a fractional value, rather than an integer division, which would round down the result and more than likely yield a result of 0. Finally, the code prints out the percentage of turns in which the player's score increased, helping Alex analyze whether the game's randomness is balanced.

Text Box 5.1 shows the last few lines from the results of the test run. After 10,000 simulations, the code is increasing the player's score about

63% of the time, which is in line with what Alex deems to be a fair and balanced game.

Text Box 5.1: Test Case 1 Sample Output

After 10000 simulations:
The player's score increased 6287 times.
This is 62.87% of the total turns.

Test Case 2: Validating the Enum for Resource Types

Next, Alex needs to confirm that the updated Resource class and ResourceType enum work as expected. While the current version of the game is only collecting wood, it's important to ensure that the code can be extended to handle different resource types, such as stone or steel, in future updates.

Code Block 5.6: Additional Code for PlayTurn

```
1 Console.WriteLine($"You collected: {resource.Type}");
```

Alex realizes that his current implementation of the PlayTurn method doesn't display which resource type the player has collected. Without this information, it's impossible to confirm that the correct resource type is being used when the player collects resources. To address this, Alex decides to add a line of code in the PlayTurn method to output the collected resource type to the console. Code Block 5.6 shows the line Alex adds to the PlayTurn method, right after the resource is collected.

Text Box 5.2: Test Case 2 Sample Output

Starting a new turn...
Attempt 1/3: 44 resources.
Attempt 2/3: 35 resources.
Attempt 3/3: 39 resources.
You earned a score bonus!
Collected this turn: 118
Your score: 118
You collected: Stone
Want to play another turn (y/n)? n
Thank you for playing!

Text Box 5.2 shows the output after Alex modifies the PlayTurn method to gather ResourceType.Stone. This output confirms that the enumeration is working properly and that resource types are correctly identified and displayed in the game.

Step 5. Refine and Optimize

As Alex begins to refine his game, he realizes that adding variety to the types of resources collected could make the game more engaging. Currently, the game forces the player to collect wood each turn. To make the game play more dynamic, Alex decides to randomly select a resource type each time the player collects resources.

The challenge of course is that resources are now separate cases within the ResourceType enumeration. Alex knows how to generate a random number, but how does he convert a random number into an individual ResourceType? To implement this random selection of resource types, Alex needs to first modify the ResourceType enumeration to include a **backing value** for each resource type. Code Block 5.7 shows how Alex updates the ResourceType enumeration.

Code Block 5.7: Revised ResourceType Enumeration

```
1  public enum ResourceType
2  {
3      Wood = 0, Stone = 1, Steel = 2, Graphite = 3
4  }
```

With this change, each resource type now explicitly corresponds to an integer, with wood assigned to 0, stone to 1, and so on. This makes it easier to use a random number generator to select one of these values.

Code Block 5.8 shows how Alex updates the PlayTurn method to incorporate random resource selection. He uses the Next() method to generate a random number between 0 and the total number of resource types in the ResourceType enumeration. Note that the Next() method can also work with just one parameter, but when used in this way, the parameter represents the exclusive upper bound of the range, and the method assumes that the inclusive lower bound is 0.

In line 12, Alex dynamically determines how many resource types are defined in the ResourceType enumeration. This is crucial because it allows the random number generator to produce a valid index within the range of the enumeration backing values.

Code Block 5.8: Revised PlayTurn Method

```
1  public void PlayTurn()
2  {
3    int turnTotal = 0;
4    for (int i = 0; i < maxAttempts; i++)
5    {
6      int attemptTotal = random.Next(20, 51);
7      turnTotal += attemptTotal;
8      Console.Write($"Attempt {i + 1}/{maxAttempts}: ");
9      Console.WriteLine($"{attemptTotal} resources.");
10   }
11   // Randomly select a resource type
12   int maxIndex = Enum.GetValues(typeof(ResourceType)).Length;
13   int resourceIndex = random.Next(maxIndex);
14   ResourceType selectedResource = (ResourceType)resourceIndex;
15
16   // Collect resources of the randomly selected type
17   Resource resource = new(selectedResource, turnTotal);
18   Player.CollectResource(resource);
19   Console.WriteLine($"Collected this turn: {turnTotal}");
20   Console.WriteLine($"Your score: {Player.Score}");
21   Console.WriteLine($"You collected: {resource.Type}");
22 }
```

The typeof keyword in C# is used to obtain the Type object for a specific C# type. By passing typeof(ResourceType) to the GetValues() method, Alex is telling the program to retrieve a set of all possible values defined within the ResourceType enumeration.

The GetValues() method is a static method in the Enum class. The Enum class provides helper functions for working with enumerations. In this case, the method returns all the values defined in the ResourceType enumeration, such as Wood, Stone, Steel, and Graphite. By appending Length to the end, Alex retrieves the total number of items in the enumeration.

After determining the randomly selected resource type, the game then creates a new Resource object, using the selected ResourceType and the total number of resources collected during the turn (line 17). This Resource object is passed to the player's CollectResource method, which determines if the player receives a score bonus (line 18).

Finally, the method provides immediate feedback to the player by displaying both the total number of resources collected and the specific resource type (lines 19 through 21). This gives the player clear information about their progress and adds an element of surprise, as they never know in advance which resource they will end up collecting.

Recap: Establish Boundaries with Purpose

As Alex worked through this chapter, he applied the problem-solving strategy of Establishing Boundaries with Purpose to ensure that his game was well-organized, secure, and balanced. By carefully defining both the scope and lifetime of variables, Alex protected critical parts of the program from unintended access or manipulation, while ensuring that variables were available for as long as they were needed and no longer. He also added unpredictability in a controlled way, using randomness to keep the game engaging while maintaining balance. Finally, Alex introduced enumerations to categorize and manage related values like resource types, ensuring consistency throughout the game.

By defining boundaries with purpose, Alex's game became more efficient, robust, and easier to manage. This strategy reminds us that setting clear boundaries allows us to steward our resources wisely. Let's add Establishing Boundaries with Purpose to your growing problem-solving toolkit in Text Box 5.3.

Summary

In this chapter, Alex took on the challenge of incorporating randomness and structure into his game, focusing on key concepts such as variable scope and lifetime, the use of randomness, and enumerations. Just as boundaries in life help us manage resources and navigate the unexpected, Alex established boundaries in his code to organize and protect variables, while also adding unpredictability to keep the game play engaging.

Alex implemented randomness by using the Random class to vary the number of resources a player collects each turn, ensuring that the game feels fresh and unpredictable. However, randomness also brought up important considerations about managing the scope and lifetime of variables. By carefully defining where and how long the random object could be accessed (using a static variable), Alex ensured that the game's random number generation would work properly and consistently throughout the game.

Text Box 5.3: Problem-Solving Strategies

1. **Follow the Five-Step Problem-Solving Process**
   Understand the problem, plan the solution, implement the solution, test the solution, and finally refine and optimize it. This structured approach will help you systematically tackle any programming challenge you encounter.

2. **Break Down Big Problems into Smaller Parts**
   Whenever you face a large, complicated problem, break it down into smaller, simpler parts. In programming, this often involves using objects and classes to represent different pieces of the problem. By focusing on one piece at a time, you'll find the overall solution much easier to achieve.

3. **Evaluate Multiple Scenarios**
   Plan for different conditions and map out the appropriate actions for each. This includes identifying the extreme values at the edges of the expected inputs and testing how the program behaves under these conditions.

4. **Repeating with Purpose**
   When designing loops, analyze the tasks to be repeated, identifying what stays consistent (commonality) and what changes (variability) in each iteration. Be intentional about how and why you're repeating actions, and ensure that loops serve a clear purpose, stopping when the goal is achieved.

5. **Establishing Boundaries with Purpose**
   Define variable scope, lifetime, and the structure of your data thoughtfully, ensuring that your program has the right balance between protection and flexibility. Establish clear boundaries in your program's design to protect important variables and maintain control in a way that reduces errors and improves efficiency.

Additionally, Alex introduced enumerations to represent the types of resources players could collect, such as Wood, Stone, and Graphite. This change helped organize related values under a single category, reducing errors like typos and making the code easier to maintain.

The problem-solving strategy Alex employed was Establishing Boundaries with Purpose. By thinking carefully about how to control the scope, lifetime, and structure of his data, Alex improved the efficiency and clarity of his game. In programming, as in life, setting the right boundaries helps protect what matters and enables better management of resources. This chapter reinforced the importance of defining clear limits and managing both unpredictability and structure to create more robust, maintainable programs.

Through testing and refining his solution, Alex's game became more engaging and easier to maintain, demonstrating that intentional boundaries allow for better stewardship of resources, whether in code or in the gifts and responsibilities entrusted to us in life.

Review Questions

1. What is the role of variable scope in programming, and how does it help manage access to data within a program?

2. Provide an example of when you would want to restrict access to a variable using the private access specifier in an application.

3. What is the difference between the lifetime of a variable and its scope.

4. In what scenarios would you use a static variable in a class? Give an example of a program that might require a static variable and explain why.

5. How does the Random class in C# generate pseudo-random numbers, and why is it important to reuse a single instance of the random object throughout a program?

6. Describe what an enumeration is and explain how it can improve the clarity and safety of your code. Explain how an enumeration could be used in a weather application.

7. Discuss the importance of setting boundaries when designing the structure of your data, particularly when using access specifiers like public and private. How can you apply these boundaries to a personal budget-tracking app?

8. Why might randomness be useful in a non-gaming context, such as a music recommendation engine or a quiz app?

9. If you were designing a vending machine program that dispenses random prizes when a customer buys a snack, how would you use enumerations to represent different prize categories and the Random class to choose a random prize?

10. How does casting help ensure that the results of an operation are accurate when working with different data types, such as integers and doubles? Provide an example of when casting would be necessary in a calculator program.

Practice Problems

1. **Employee Payroll System**. Create an Employee class with properties for Name, HoursWorked, and HourlyWage. Use private variables to ensure that the total pay is only calculated internally and implement a method that returns the total pay after hours and wages have been set.

2. **University Enrollment**. Design a University class that keeps track of how many students have enrolled using a private static variable. The class should also have a method that enrolls a student by incrementing this variable. Include a second method that displays the total number of enrolled students.

3. **Game High Score Tracker**. Implement a simple Game class that tracks the high-score for a game. Use a static variable to track the highest score submitted. Use a method to submit a new high score, and each time a new score is submitted, check if it is higher than the current highest score. If so, update the static high-score variable.

4. **Weather Forecast Generator**. Write a program that generates a random 7-day weather forecast. Use the Random class to select different weather types (sunny, rainy, cloudy, etc.) and display the result for each day. Use an enumeration to represent the different weather types. Make sure the random object is created once with the appropriate scope and lifetime.

5. **Coffee Shop Menu**. Create an enumeration called `CoffeeSize` that represents different sizes of coffee (Small, Medium, Large). Write a `CoffeeOrder` class that uses this enumeration to store the size of the coffee. Add a method that allows the user to select a size, stores the size in the class, and prints out a message based on the user's selection.

6. **Car Rental Service**. Create an enumeration called `CarType` that represents different categories of rental cars (Economy, Sedan, SUV, etc.). Write a `CarRental` class that uses this enumeration to store the selected car type. Add a method that allows the customer to select a car type, stores the selection in the class, and outputs the car type to the console.

7. **Item Generator**. Create an enumeration called `ItemType` that represents different types of items a player can collect (Sword, Shield, Helmet, etc.). Write an `ItemGenerator` class that uses this enumeration to store the randomly selected item type. Add a method that generates a random item by selecting both an `ItemType` and a random strength value (1-100). Store the generated item in the class and display a message showing the collected item type and its strength.

8. **Workout Routine Generator**. Write a fitness program that randomly selects a workout routine for a user. Use an enumeration `WorkoutType` to represent different types of workouts (Cardio, Strength, Yoga, etc.). Randomly generate the workout type and duration (between 20 and 60 minutes) for the user's daily workout routine and display the results.

"You will surely wear yourselves out, both you and these people who are with you. For the task is too heavy for you; you cannot do it alone"
Exodus 18:18 (ESV)

CHAPTER 6

DELEGATING BEHAVIOR WITH METHODS

Introduction

Throughout the Bible, we see numerous examples of godly leadership and wisdom when it comes to delegating responsibilities. God, in His infinite wisdom, often entrusted people with specific jobs to carry out His plans. Delegation is not only central to spiritual leadership but also deeply woven into the fabric of effective problem-solving.

One of the most powerful illustrations of delegation in Scripture is found in the life of Moses. When the Israelites left Egypt and began their journey through the wilderness, Moses initially attempted to handle all disputes and leadership responsibilities himself. However, his father-in-law, Jethro, observed how this burden was overwhelming Moses and offered wise counsel. He said to Moses, "You will surely wear yourselves out, both you and these people who are with you. For the task is too heavy for you; you cannot do it alone" (Exodus 18:18 ESV).

Jethro advised Moses to appoint capable men to share the leadership load, delegating authority and responsibility. While Moses would continue to oversee the most important matters, others would be assigned simpler tasks. By delegating wisely, Moses was able to focus on the critical responsibilities of leadership while allowing others to handle the smaller disputes. This empowered the entire community to function more effectively.

The Apostle Paul builds on this idea of delegation in his letters to the early church. In 1 Corinthians 12:12-31, Paul compares the Church to the human body, emphasizing that each part has a unique function. No part can say to another, "I don't need you." Just as the body thrives when each part carries out its role, so too the Church functions at its best when every member fulfills their God-given responsibility. Every person plays an essential part, and when responsibilities are delegated according to each member's gifts, the body operates in unity and harmony.

The principles of delegation found in Scripture offer insight into how we approach programming. Just as Moses learned the importance of delegating tasks to others, we must learn how to delegate behavior and responsibilities within our programs. In object-oriented programming, this is accomplished through methods. When we design programs, we distribute responsibilities across different objects and classes, much like how a wise leader delegates tasks to capable team members.

In this chapter, we'll explore this concept of delegating behavior through methods. To delegate well, we must decide carefully which class is responsible for which behavior in our code. We'll introduce a new problem-solving strategy called the Expert Pattern to help guide us in assigning behavior to the correct class.

Furthermore, we must ensure that each class and method in our program serves a specific and useful purpose. Methods allow us to encapsulate behavior in a way that makes our programs more modular and maintainable. By breaking down complex tasks into smaller, manageable methods, we mirror the biblical model of delegation, ensuring that our code is both efficient and easy to manage.

Finally, we'll look at lambda expressions, which allow us to delegate behavior while maintaining some control over how that behavior is carried out. In programming, there are situations where we want to hand off responsibility for a task but still provide some guidance on how that task should be completed. Lambda expressions enable us to pass behavior into methods in a concise and flexible way, offering a balance between delegation and control.

By applying the biblical principles of delegation and leadership to our approach to programming, we not only become better problem solvers but also more intentional in how we structure our code. Whether in life or coding, wise delegation helps ensure that each part functions effectively.

Step 1. Understand the Problem

As Alex continues to expand his game, he realizes that the mechanics are becoming more complex, and managing the growing responsibilities of each part of the game is starting to feel overwhelming. Initially, it was easy enough for him to manage tasks like resource collection and score calculation within a few simple methods, but now, with the introduction of additional game play features, Alex is beginning to see that his code needs to be more organized and maintainable.

He knows he wants to introduce a system where players can level up as they collect resources. Players will gain experience points (XP) with each successful resource collection. When they reach a certain XP threshold, they should have the option to level up. With each new level, their maximum stamina will increase, allowing them to collect more resources before needing to recharge. Managing this increase in player stamina with leveling up will add depth to the game and give players more control over how they progress. However, Alex also knows that players should have the option to spend their XP strategically. If they level up too quickly, they could run out of stamina during their turn, and potentially lose the game.

Alex decides that players should have a few options at the beginning of each turn: they can choose to either collect resources, restore stamina, level up, or quit the game. This decision-making process will give players more control over their progress, but it also means that the code needs to be flexible enough to handle different outcomes based on the player's choices.

At the same time, Alex wants to introduce an efficient way to handle specific calculations for score bonuses during resource collection. For example, score bonuses are currently handled in the CollectResource method in the Player class, but Alex would like the Game class to share the responsibility of determining how much of a bonus to give the player based on their collected resource type. Using lambda expressions will allow him to accomplish this behavior.

With these new mechanics, Alex recognizes that managing all this logic in one place could quickly become unwieldy. Each part of the game needs to be carefully organized and separated into different responsibilities. Alex knows that he needs to delegate each of these responsibilities to the right parts of the game to ensure that everything runs correctly and that the code is easy to maintain.

As Alex thinks through these changes, he realizes that delegation is important to keeping the game organized and scalable. He needs a system where tasks are assigned to the right place, whether that means creating new methods, using lambda expressions, or delegating existing responsibility to different classes. Alex is now ready to move on to planning how he'll structure these new mechanics in his game.

Step 2. Plan the Solution

As Alex considers how to implement a player leveling system, stamina management, and a more flexible resource collection process, it's clear that he needs to break these responsibilities into manageable pieces. Alex begins by adding a menu system that will allow the player to make key decisions at the start of each turn. This menu will give players four options: collecting resources, restoring stamina, leveling up, or quitting the game. Rather than hard coding the logic for this menu directly into the main game loop, Alex wants to delegate the responsibility of displaying the menu and processing the player's choice to a separate method. But Alex still needs to determine which class should contain this new method. This is where the Expert Pattern strategy can help. The Expert Pattern advises that any new behavior should be placed in the class that knows the most about how to carry out the behavior (i.e., the expert class on the behavior). The easiest way to see which class is the expert for any behavior is to look at the class diagram. The class that has the most properties, methods, and direct relationship properties related to the behavior is the expert for that behavior. As Alex reviews the class diagram, he sees that the Game class contains the turn related properties as well as a **relationship property** for the Player class, which is everything that the menu system will need to operate. Alex concludes that the expert class for the menu behavior is the Game class.

To keep the code even cleaner, Alex plans to ensure that the game has individual methods that handle each menu option. For example, the game should have a dedicated method for collecting resources, another method for restoring stamina, and another for leveling up. The main game loop will simply call the appropriate method based on the player's menu choice. This separation of responsibilities will keep the game's structure clear and maintainable. The key is to ensure that each method is

---

Text Box 6.1: Menu System Pseudo-code

While the game is still running:
  Show the player a menu with the following choices:
    1. Collect resources
    2. Restore stamina
    3. Level up
    4. Quit the game
  Ask the player to enter one of the four options.
  If the player selects "Collect resources":
    Call the method that allows them to gather resources.
  If the player selects "Restore stamina":
    Call the method to help them regain stamina.
  If the player selects "Level up":
    Call the method that lets them increase their level if they have enough experience.
  If the player selects "Quit":
    End the game.
  If the player enters an invalid choice:
    Display a message saying, "Invalid choice. Please select option 1, 2, 3, or 4."
Repeat the process until the player chooses to quit the game.

responsible for only one thing, so that the code remains flexible as new mechanics are added in the future.

To make sure Alex's plan is clear before moving forward with implementation, it's helpful to break down the structure of his approach in a way that's easy to visualize and refine. This is where pseudo-code or an activity diagram can play an important role in the planning process. For example, the pseudo-code for the player's menu system might look something like Text Box 6.1.

Next, Alex needs to think about the player's leveling system. When a player collects resources, they will gain experience points (XP). Once they reach a certain XP threshold, they should be able to level up, which increases their maximum stamina. If the player chooses to "Level Up" from the menu, the game should check whether they have enough XP to level up and, if so, increase their level and stamina accordingly.

Text Box 6.2: Pseudo-code for XP and Stamina Management

When the player selects the "Level Up" option:
    Check the player's XP.
    If the XP is greater than or equal to the required XP for the next level:
        Increase the player's level by 1.
        Increase the player's maximum stamina.
        Subtract the required XP from the player's XP.
When the player selects the "Restore Stamina" option:
    Check the player's XP.
    If the player has enough XP to restore stamina:
        Deduct the required XP from the player.
        Restore stamina to the maximum level for the current player level.
After each turn, update and display the player's remaining stamina and XP.

At the same time, Alex realizes that stamina needs to be carefully managed. Collecting resources should consume stamina, meaning that if the player's stamina is too low, they won't be able to collect resources during that turn. Assuming the player has saved enough XP, the "Restore Stamina" menu option should use XP to fill their stamina to the maximum value for their level. This adds an interesting dynamic to the game, forcing players to balance the decision between leveling up and restoring stamina, as using too much XP to level up could leave them without enough stamina to continue playing. Alex plans his solution to the player leveling and stamina management systems with the pseudo-code in Text Box 6.2.

For the resource collection process itself, Alex wants to introduce a score bonus system that will vary based on the type of resource being collected. For example, collecting gold might yield a score bonus multiplier of 2, while collecting gemstones could have a multiplier of 3. Instead of hard coding this bonus system into the resource collection method, Alex decides to use a lambda expression, which will allow him to pass in the logic for calculating the bonus. This approach allows the Game class to retain control over how bonus points are calculated, but still delegates the responsibility for adding bonus points to the Player class. Alex plans the solution to the resource collection process with the pseudo-code in Text Box 6.3.

Text Box 6.3: Pseudo-code for Resource Collection

When the player collects a resource:
    Check the type of resource being collected.
    Define a bonus calculation lambda:
        If the resource type is "Gold":
            Return a multiplier of 2.
        If the resource type is "Gemstones":
            Return a multiplier of 3.
        Otherwise:
            Return a multiplier of 0.
    Pass the bonus calculation lambda to the Player class to apply the bonus:
        The Player class uses the lambda to calculate the bonus points.
        Add the bonus points to the player's score.
    After the bonus is applied:
        Display the player's total score, including any resource collection bonus.

Before we get into applying lambda expressions in Alex's game, let's take a moment to understand what a lambda expression is and how it works in C#. Lambda expressions are essentially short, inline methods that can be passed as arguments to other methods. They allow for flexible delegation of behavior without needing to define a separate method.

In C#, lambda expressions are often used alongside delegates. A delegate is a special variable type that allows a variable to hold a method instead of a traditional value. For example, if we want a method to perform different kinds of mathematical operations (like addition, subtraction, or multiplication), we can define a parameter of our method to be a delegate that will hold the method containing the operation to be performed.

One type of delegate commonly used with lambda expressions is the Func<T> delegate. The Func<T> delegate serves as a placeholder for a method that takes zero or more input parameters and returns a value. The angle brackets enclose a comma-separated list of data types for both the input parameters and the return value.

Let's walk through a simple example. Suppose we have a Mathematics class with a Calc method that takes two integers and a Func<int, int, int> as parameters. In this case, Func<int, int, int>, means we're defining a delegate parameter that accepts a method that takes two integers as input and returns an integer. Code Block 6.1 shows how this declaration would work.

Code Block 6.1: Sample Delegate Parameter

```
1| public class Mathematics
2| {
3|    public int Calc(int x, int y, Func<int, int, int> operation)
4|    {
5|       return operation(x, y);
6|    }
7| }
```

In the Calc method, the operation parameter is a Func<int, int, int> delegate. This means the operation parameter expects to be given a method with two integer parameters (the first two int's in the list) that returns an integer value (the final int in the list). However, the Calc method doesn't need to know the details of the operation itself; it just needs to execute the operation when needed.

Code Block 6.2: Lambda Expression Syntax

```
1| (input parameters) => expression
```

This is where lambda expressions come in handy. A lambda expression provides a concise way to define the operation at the time we call the Calc method. The basic syntax of a lambda expression is shown in Code Block 6.2.

This method allows us to pass different behaviors into Calc depending on the lambda we use. In this case, since we are working with a Func<int, int, int> delegate, we could use Calc to add, subtract, or multiply two numbers, as shown in Code Block 6.3.

Code Block 6.3: Sample Use of Lambda Expressions

```
 1| Mathematics math = new();
 2| // Add two numbers
 3| int result1 = math.Calc(5, 10, (a, b) => a + b);
 4| Console.WriteLine(result1);   // Output: 15
 5|
 6| // Subtract two numbers
 7| int result2 = math.Calc(20, 8, (a, b) => a - b);
 8| Console.WriteLine(result2);   // Output: 12
 9|
10| // Multiply two numbers
11| int result3 = math.Calc(4, 6, (a, b) => a * b);
12| Console.WriteLine(result3);   // Output: 24
```

In each example, the lambda expression (a, b) => a + b (or a - b or a * b) defines how the two integers passed into the Calc method should be processed. The Calc method remains generic and reusable because it delegates the specific behavior to the lambda expression passed in as an argument.

By using lambda expressions, Alex can delegate behavior to methods while still retaining flexibility over how certain tasks should be performed. Instead of writing a separate method for every possible calculation or task, Alex can use lambda expressions to inject bonus calculation logic into the CollectResource method. This helps keep the code concise, flexible, and maintainable.

Before Alex moves forward with implementing the code, he first updates the class diagram to include the necessary methods, fields, and properties for his solution. The updated diagram is shown in Figure 6.1.

Step 3. Implement the Solution

Now that Alex has a clear plan in place, it's time to start implementing the new mechanics into his game. We'll begin by adding the menu system that

Figure 6.1: Updated Class Diagram

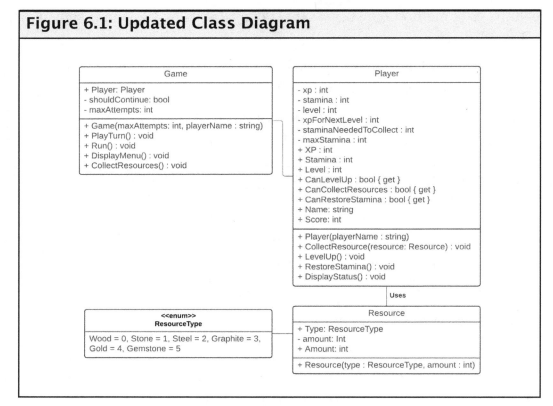

allows the player to choose from various actions, followed by methods to handle those actions.

Implementing the Menu System

To give players control over their actions each turn, Alex needs to design a menu system that offers the player four choices: collect resources, restore stamina, level up, or quit the game. Rather than hard coding the logic for this menu directly into the game loop, Alex decides to delegate the task of displaying the menu and collecting the player's choice to its own method in the Game class. Code Block 6.4 shows how Alex accomplishes that.

With this DisplayMenu method, Alex has created a simple yet effective way to let players decide their next action. The method keeps prompting the player until they enter a valid option. By separating this logic from the rest of the game, Alex has not only made his code more modular but also easier to update if more options are added later.

Code Block 6.4: DisplayMenu Method

```
1  public class Game
2  {
3    private static Random random = new();
4    private bool shouldContinue;
5    private int maxAttempts;
6    public Player Player { get; set; }
7
8    public Game(int maxAttempts, string playerName)
9    {
10     this.maxAttempts = maxAttempts;
11     shouldContinue = true;
12     Player = new(playerName);
13   }
14   // Method to display the menu and get player's choice
15   public int DisplayMenu()
16   {
17     int choice;
18     do
19     {
20       Console.WriteLine("Choose an option:");
21       Console.WriteLine("1. Collect Resources");
22       Console.WriteLine("2. Restore Stamina");
23       Console.WriteLine("3. Level Up");
24       Console.WriteLine("4. Quit");
25       string input = Console.ReadLine();
26       bool isValid = int.TryParse(input, out choice);
27
28       if (!isValid || choice < 1 || choice > 4)
29       {
30         Console.WriteLine("Please enter a number between 1 and 4.");
31       }
32     } while (choice < 1 || choice > 4);
33     return choice;
34   }
35   // Other methods here...
36 }
```

Handling Player Actions with Methods

Next, Alex needs to handle each of the menu choices with dedicated methods. By delegating the responsibilities for leveling up, restoring stamina, and collecting resources to their own methods, Alex can keep the main game loop clean and focused on making the game flow from one action to the next.

To handle the player's XP and stamina correctly, Alex realizes that he needs to add several new properties and a DisplayStatus method to the Player class, since the player is the expert of leveling up. From his previous experience with the Amount property, Alex has learned that he should use full properties to prevent stamina or XP from dropping below zero, and he also needs to ensure that stamina does not exceed the maximum stamina allowed for the player's level. Code Block 6.5 shows how Alex revises the Player class to implement the additional properties and method needed.

Code Block 6.5: Updated Player Class

```
 1| public class Player
 2| {
 3|   private int xp;
 4|   private int stamina;
 5|   private int level;
 6|   private int xpForNextLevel;
 7|   private int maxStamina;
 8|
 9|   public int XP
10|   {
11|       get { return xp; }
12|       set { xp = value < 0 ? 0 : value; }
13|   }
14|
15|   public int Stamina
16|   {
17|     get { return stamina; }
18|     set
19|     {
20|       stamina = value < 0 ? 0 : value > maxStamina ? maxStamina : value;
21|     }
22|   }
23|
24|   public int Level
25|   {
26|     get { return level; }
27|     set { level = value < 0 ? 0 : value; }
28|   }
29|
30|   public Player(string playerName)
31|   {
32|     Name = playerName;
33|     Score = 0;
34|     XP = 0;
35|     maxStamina = 100;
36|     Stamina = 100;
37|     Level = 1;
38|     xpForNextLevel = 100;
39|   }
40|
41|   // Method to display the player's current status
42|   public void DisplayStatus()
43|   {
44|     Console.WriteLine($"Player Status:");
45|     Console.WriteLine($"Level: {Level}");
46|     Console.WriteLine($"XP: {XP}");
47|     Console.WriteLine($"Stamina: {Stamina}/{maxStamina}");
48|     Console.WriteLine($"Score: {Score}");
49|   }
50|
51|
52|   // Other properties and methods of the Player class...
53|
54| }
```

In this revised code, Alex uses the ternary operator in the XP property to ensure that its value cannot go below zero (line 12). For the Stamina property, Alex uses two ternary operators to first verify if the incoming value is less than 0 (line 20). If it is, then stamina is set to 0; otherwise, the value is checked to see if it is greater than the maximum stamina allowed. If it is greater than the maximum, then stamina is set to maxStamina; otherwise, it is set to the incoming value.

Leveling Up

Next, Alex turns his attention to implementing the leveling up functionality. Following the Expert Pattern, Alex knows that the Player class is the expert on behaviors related to player progression, so he decides to place the LevelUp method in the Player class. Alex also creates a computed property with just a get accessor to determine if the player has enough XP to level up. He uses a **computed property** for this, because he senses that this could be a common question that the Player class would need to answer. The LevelUp method and the CanLevelUp property are shown in Code Block 6.6.

Code Block 6.6: LevelUp Method and CanLevelUp Property

```
 1| public bool CanLevelUp
 2| {
 3|    get { return XP >= xpForNextLevel; }
 4| }
 5|
 6| public void LevelUp()
 7| {
 8|    if (CanLevelUp)
 9|    {
10|       Level++;
11|       XP -= xpForNextLevel;
12|       maxStamina += 10;
13|       Console.WriteLine("You leveled up! Max stamina increased.");
14|    }
15|    else
16|    {
17|       Console.WriteLine("You don't have enough XP to level up.");
18|    }
19| }
```

The LevelUp method checks whether the player has enough XP to level up, and if so, it increases their level and maximum stamina, while reducing their XP.

Collecting Resources

Currently, all the logic for collecting resources resides within the PlayTurn method in the Game class. Since Alex has expanded the player's available options each turn, he decides that now is a good time to refactor the resource collection code into its own method within the Game class, making the code cleaner and more modular. This new CollectResources method will continue to work with the existing CollectResource method in the Player class. However, the CollectResource method will now be modified to accept a Func<int> delegate, which will determine how the bonus score is calculated when collecting different types of resources. Code Block 6.7 shows Alex's updated CollectResources method, as well as a new CanCollectResources computed property in the Player class.

Code Block 6.7: Updated CollectResource with Func Delegate

```
 1| public bool CanCollectResources
 2| {
 3|   get { return Stamina >= staminaNeededToCollect; }
 4| }
 5|
 6| public void CollectResource(Resource resource, Func<int> bonus)
 7| {
 8|   if (CanCollectResources) {
 9|     // Decision logic based on the collected resources
10|     switch (resource.Amount)
11|     {
12|       case >= 100:
13|         Score += resource.Amount * bonus();
14|         Console.WriteLine("You earned a score bonus!");
15|         break;
16|       case >= 50:
17|         Console.WriteLine("Good job! You're halfway there.");
18|         break;
19|       case 0:
20|         Console.WriteLine("No resources collected.");
21|         break;
22|       default:
23|         Console.WriteLine("Keep going to reach your goal.");
24|         break;
25|     }
26|     Stamina -= staminaNeededToCollect;
27|   }
28|   else
29|   {
30|     Console.WriteLine("Not enough stamina to collect resources!");
31|   }
32| }
```

In the updated CollectResource method, Alex introduces a Func<int> delegate named bonus, which allows the calling method to determine separately how the bonus score is calculated (line 6). When the resource amount reaches 100 or more, the method adds to the player's score a bonus equal to the collected resource amount multiplied by the result from calling the bonus() method (line 13).

The Game class will need to pass in a lambda expression that defines the logic for calculating the bonus multiplier, giving control to the Game class while keeping the Player class responsible for the actual resource collection. Code Block 6.8 shows how Alex creates the CollectResources method in the Game class.

Code Block 6.8: Updated CollectResources in the Game Class

```
1  public void CollectResources()
2  {
3    if (Player.CanCollectResources)
4    {
5      int turnTotal = 0;
6      for (int i = 0; i < maxAttempts; i++)
7      {
8        int attemptTotal = random.Next(20, 51);
9        turnTotal += attemptTotal;
10        Console.Write($"Attempt {i + 1}/{maxAttempts}: ");
11        Console.WriteLine($"{attemptTotal} resources.");
12      }
13
14      // Randomly select a resource type
15      int maxIndex = Enum.GetValues(typeof(ResourceType)).Length;
16      int resourceIndex = random.Next(maxIndex);
17      ResourceType selectedResource = (ResourceType)resourceIndex;
18
19      // Collect resources of the randomly selected type
20      Resource resource = new(selectedResource, turnTotal);
21
22      Player.CollectResource(resource, () => {
23        // Define the function that will be passed to the delegate parameter
24        switch (selectedResource)
25        {
26          case ResourceType.Gold:
27            return 2;
28          case ResourceType.Gemstone:
29            return 3;
30          default:
31            return 1;
32        }
33      });
34      Console.WriteLine($"Collected this turn: {turnTotal}");
35      Console.WriteLine($"Your score: {Player.Score}");
36      Console.WriteLine($"You collected: {resource.Type}");
37    }
38    else
39    {
40      Console.WriteLine("Insufficient Stamina to Collect Resources!");
41    }
42  }
```

In the updated `CollectResources` method, Alex passes a lambda expression to the player's `CollectResource` method (lines 22 through 33), allowing the `Game` class to control how the score bonus is calculated based on the type of resource collected. The lambda expression evaluates the selected resource type, applying different score multipliers depending on whether the player collects gold, gemstones, or other resources. If the selected resource is gold, the lambda returns a bonus multiplier of 2 (lines 26 and 27), and if it is a gemstone, the multiplier is 3 (lines 28 and 29). All other resources receive a default multiplier of 1 (lines 30 and 31).

By using this lambda expression, Alex ensures that the `Game` class has flexibility in determining how the score bonuses are applied, while the `Player` class only focuses on managing the actual resource collection. This keeps the `Player` class more focused, while allowing the `Game` class to easily update or extend the bonus system logic in the future if new resource types are added or if the bonus logic changes.

Restoring Stamina

In addition to managing resource collection and leveling up, Alex implements a system to handle stamina restoration in the game. As the player collects resources, their stamina decreases. If stamina drops too low, the player will be unable to collect more resources. To prevent the player from being stuck without stamina, Alex adds the `RestoreStamina` method shown in Code Block 6.9, which allows the player to spend their unused XP to refill their stamina.

The computed property `CanRestoreStamina` is used to determine whether the player has enough XP to restore their stamina to the maximum value. This property checks whether the player's available XP is greater than or equal to the difference between their maximum stamina and their current stamina (line 3). If the player has enough XP, they can restore stamina by using the `RestoreStamina` method.

When the `RestoreStamina` method is called, it first checks `CanRestoreStamina` (line 8). If the player has enough XP, it calculates the cost of restoring stamina (based on the difference between max stamina and current stamina) and deducts the corresponding amount of XP (lines 10 and 11). The player's stamina is then fully restored to the max value (line 12), and the player receives a message indicating how much XP was used (line 13). If the player doesn't have enough XP, they are notified that they can't restore their stamina (line 17).

Code Block 6.9: RestoreStamina Method in the Player Class

```
 1| public bool CanRestoreStamina
 2| {
 3|   get { return XP >= maxStamina - Stamina; }
 4| }
 5|
 6| public void RestoreStamina()
 7| {
 8|   if (CanRestoreStamina)
 9|   {
10|     int costToRestore = maxStamina - Stamina;
11|     XP -= costToRestore;
12|     Stamina = maxStamina;
13|     Console.WriteLine($"Stamina restored! {costToRestore} XP used.");
14|   }
15|   else
16|   {
17|     Console.WriteLine("Not enough XP to restore stamina!");
18|   }
19| }
```

The only thing left for Alex to implement is the new logic for the PlayTurn method, but because Alex has properly delegated all the key behaviors to separate methods, this method is very easy to write. Code Block 6.10 shows how Alex revised the PlayTurn method in the Game class. The PlayTurn method handles the flow of each turn by displaying the player's status (line 4), showing a menu to gather input (line 6), and then executing the appropriate action based on the player's choice (lines 7-22). By using a switch statement, Alex keeps the logic straightforward and easy to follow, as each action is clearly separated and calls a specific method that handles that part of the game. With all these elements in place, the next step is to test the solution.

Step 4. Test the Solution

The main areas that need to be tested include the new menu system, resource collection with the bonus multiplier, player leveling up, and stamina restoration. Each of these systems relies on proper delegation of responsibilities between the Game and Player classes, so the tests should verify that the flow of control between these classes works correctly.

Code Block 6.10: Revised PlayTurn Method in the Game Class

```
public void PlayTurn()
{
    // Show player's status before each action
    Player.DisplayStatus();
    // Display the menu and get the player's choice
    int choice = DisplayMenu();
    switch (choice)
    {
        case 1:
            CollectResources();
            break;
        case 2:
            Player.RestoreStamina();
            break;
        case 3:
            Player.LevelUp();
            break;
        case 4:
            Console.WriteLine("Thanks for playing!");
            shouldContinue = false;
            break;
    }
}
```

Testing the Menu System

The first step is to test the DisplayMenu method in the Game class. We need to verify that the menu works correctly, continues to prompt the player until a valid choice is made, and properly delegates the selected action to the corresponding method in the Game class or Player class.

To do this, Alex runs the game, enters invalid input (like letters or out-of-range numbers), and checks that the game repeatedly asks for a valid input. Once he provides valid input, the appropriate method should be called based on the player's choice. After each valid choice, Alex checks that the player's status (XP, stamina, level, and score) is updated accordingly and that the player can choose another action in the next turn.

During testing, Alex realizes that the player isn't earning any XP when successfully collecting resources. To fix this, he decides to award

1/5th of any score bonus as XP. Code Block 6.11 shows Alex's revised CollectResource method in the Player class (see line 10).

Code Block 6.11: Updated CollectResource Method in Player

```
 1| public void CollectResource(Resource resource, Func<int> bonus)
 2| {
 3|   if (CanCollectResources)
 4|   {
 5|     switch (resource.Amount)
 6|     {
 7|       case >= 100:
 8|         int bonusPoints = resource.Amount * bonus();
 9|         Score += bonusPoints;
10|         XP += bonusPoints / 5;
11|         Console.WriteLine("You earned a score bonus!");
12|         break;
13|       case >= 50:
14|         Console.WriteLine("Good job! You're halfway there.");
15|         break;
16|       case 0:
17|         Console.WriteLine("No resources collected.");
18|         break;
19|       default:
20|         Console.WriteLine("Keep going to reach your goal.");
21|         break;
22|     }
23|     Stamina -= staminaNeededToCollect;
24|   }
25|   else
26|   {
27|     Console.WriteLine("Not enough stamina to collect resources!");
28|   }
29| }
```

Testing Resource Collection with the Bonus Multiplier

Next, Alex tests the resource collection process to ensure that the correct bonus is applied based on the type of resource collected. In this test, the game should randomly select a resource type (gold, gemstones, or other resources), and the lambda expression passed to the CollectResource method in the Player class should determine the bonus multiplier.

To test this, Alex runs several turns of the game, collects different types of resources, and verifies that the correct bonus multiplier is applied for each resource type. Alex checks the player's score after each turn to ensure that the score reflects the proper bonus. Additionally, he confirms that the player's stamina is decremented after each resource collection attempt, ensuring that stamina management works as intended.

Testing Player Leveling Up

The next step is to test the leveling up system. As the player collects resources, they gain XP. Once they reach the required XP threshold, they should be able to level up, which increases their maximum stamina and level while reducing their XP.

To test this, Alex plays several turns, allowing the player to accumulate enough XP to level up. He chooses the "Level Up" option from the menu and verifies that:

- The player's level increases by 1.
- The player's maximum stamina increases.
- The required XP is subtracted from the player's XP.
- The game displays a message confirming the level-up and the increase in stamina.

Alex also tests what happens when the player selects the "Level Up" option without having enough XP. In this case, the game should display a message stating that the player does not have enough XP to level up, and the player's level and stamina should remain unchanged.

Testing Stamina Restoration

Finally, Alex tests the stamina restoration system. As the player collects resources, their stamina decreases. If their stamina gets too low, they won't be able to collect resources until they restore it. The player can restore stamina by spending their unused XP.

Alex plays the game until he has low stamina and enough XP to restore it. He selects the "Restore Stamina" option from the menu and verifies that:

- The player's stamina is restored to the maximum value allowed for their level.
- The correct amount of XP is subtracted based on how much stamina was restored.
- The game displays a message confirming how much XP was used to restore stamina.

Next, Alex tests what happens when the player tries to restore stamina without enough XP. The game should display a message stating that the player does not have enough XP to restore stamina, and the player's stamina and XP should remain unchanged. With testing complete and everything working correctly, Alex can confidently move forward with further improvements to the game.

Step 5. Refine and Optimize

While the game functions correctly, there are always opportunities to make the code more efficient, easier to maintain, and more user-friendly. By taking the time to refine the existing systems, Alex can ensure that his game remains scalable as new features are added and that it offers a smooth game play experience for the player.

As Alex considers future expansions to the game, he also looks for ways to optimize his code for scalability. He anticipates that as the game grows, he may want to add more resource types, new actions for the player to take, or even additional features like an inventory system. Alex reviews his existing methods to ensure that they are flexible and modular.

For instance, the `CollectResource` method is already set up to handle different resource types, but Alex makes sure the system is built in a way that easily supports new resource types without requiring major changes to the rest of the game. Alex also reviews the lambda expression used for calculating bonuses and ensures that it is flexible enough to accommodate future changes to the bonus system. If new resources are added later, the lambda expression can be easily updated or replaced without affecting other parts of the game.

Alex is content for now that his solution meets his current needs for the game, but it was good for Alex to take one last tour through is code to think about the future. Rather than stopping at a solution that merely works, we should push further to make the solution efficient, elegant, and ready for the next set of challenges. Now, with a robust and optimized system in place, Alex is ready to take the game to new heights as he continues adding exciting features and mechanics.

Recap: The Expert Pattern

As Alex progressed through this chapter, he applied the Expert Pattern, a problem-solving strategy that emphasizes assigning responsibility to the part of the system that has the most knowledge about how a task should be carried out. This approach ensures that the right methods are placed within the right classes, keeping the system organized and each class responsible for its specific duties. By delegating tasks to the appropriate "experts," Alex ensures that each class and method focuses on what it does best, making the code more modular, maintainable, and scalable.

In this chapter, Alex learned how to delegate responsibility by using methods to divide up the game's logic. Each method was responsible for one task, such as handling resource collection, managing stamina, or leveling up. The Expert Pattern allowed Alex to carefully place each of these tasks within the class that had the most knowledge and control over them, ensuring that his game was well-structured and easy to extend.

He also explored lambda expressions to delegate behavior while maintaining control over specific details. By using lambdas, Alex allowed the `CollectResource` method to handle the resource collection, while passing in a lambda that determined the bonus multiplier used to calculate the addition to the player's score. This flexibility allowed Alex to delegate most of the task to the `Resource` class, while allowing the `Game` class to maintain control over how the bonus was calculated.

The menu system also demonstrated the power of the Expert Pattern. Rather than handling player input and decision-making directly within the game loop, Alex delegated the responsibility for displaying the menu and processing player choices to a dedicated method in the `Game` class. Let's add the Expert Pattern to your growing problem-solving toolkit in Text Box 6.4.

Text Box 6.4: Problem-Solving Strategies

1. **Follow the Five-Step Problem-Solving Process**

   Understand the problem, plan the solution, implement the solution, test the solution, and finally refine and optimize it. This structured approach will help you systematically tackle any programming challenge you encounter.

2. **Break Down Big Problems into Smaller Parts**

   Whenever you face a large, complicated problem, break it down into smaller, simpler parts. In programming, this often involves using objects and classes to represent different pieces of the problem. By focusing on one piece at a time, you'll find the overall solution much easier to achieve.

3. **Evaluate Multiple Scenarios**

   Plan for different conditions and map out the appropriate actions for each. This includes identifying the extreme values at the edges of the expected inputs and testing how the program behaves under these conditions.

4. **Repeating with Purpose**

   When designing loops, analyze the tasks to be repeated, identifying what stays consistent (commonality) and what changes (variability) in each iteration. Be intentional about how and why you're repeating actions, and ensure that loops serve a clear purpose, stopping when the goal is achieved.

5. **Establishing Boundaries with Purpose**

   Define variable scope, lifetime, and the structure of your data thoughtfully, ensuring that your program has the right balance between protection and flexibility. Establish clear boundaries in your program's design to protect important variables and maintain control in a way that reduces errors and improves efficiency.

6. **The Expert Pattern**

   Assign responsibility for tasks to the classes or methods that have the most knowledge and control over the task. By delegating behavior to the "experts" in your system, you ensure that your code is well-organized, each piece is responsible for its own duties, and the program remains modular and easy to manage. Use the Expert Pattern to decide where each method belongs and ensure that your code is clear, maintainable, and adaptable as the system grows.

Summary

In this chapter, we explored the concept of delegation in programming, focusing on how to assign responsibility for different tasks to the most appropriate parts of the code. We introduced the Expert Pattern, a strategy for assigning tasks to the classes or methods best suited to handle them, which helps keep the code organized, modular, and easy to manage.

We began by defining the game play mechanics that Alex wanted to implement: a menu system to give players options each turn, a player leveling system that increases stamina, and a resource collection system that applies a score bonus based on the type of resource collected. The focus was on how to effectively delegate these tasks across multiple methods and classes to ensure each part of the system is responsible for its own behavior.

We also introduced lambda expressions to delegate behavior while retaining flexibility. Lambdas allow us to pass behavior as an argument to methods, so that we can customize how a method executes certain parts of its task. In Alex's game, lambdas were used to delegate the responsibility for calculating score bonuses during resource collection. This allowed the Resource class to handle the overall collection process while the bonus calculation was passed in as a lambda, keeping the game's logic flexible and easy to modify.

Throughout the chapter, we explored the importance of breaking down tasks into manageable pieces, assigning them to the correct "experts," and ensuring that the game remained scalable as new mechanics were added.

By the end of the chapter, Alex had a fully functioning menu system that delegates player choices to individual methods, a working player leveling system that integrates with stamina management, and a flexible resource collection system that uses lambdas to apply different score bonuses based on resource types.

Review Questions

1. What is the Expert Pattern, and how does it help organize code in a way that delegates responsibility effectively?
2. What is delegation in programming, and how does it help avoid duplicating code?

3. Why is it important to delegate responsibility to the appropriate class or method, and how does this improve the maintainability of your code?

4. What is a lambda expression, and how does it allow flexibility when delegating specific behaviors to a method?

5. In a task management application, how would you structure a menu system that allows users to add, complete, and delete tasks? Why is it important to delegate these tasks to separate methods?

6. What are the advantages of using full methods for task delegation versus lambda expressions? When might you choose one over the other?

7. Describe how the Expert Pattern might interact with the Single Responsibility Principle. How can following these principles together improve the design of your application?

Practice Problems

1. **Menu System for a Task Manager**. Write a program that displays a simple menu allowing the user to choose between adding a task, marking a task as completed, or quitting the program. Delegate the logic for each action (adding, completing, and quitting) to separate methods. Make sure that invalid menu choices are handled appropriately.

2. **Basic Calculator with Lambda Expressions**. Implement a basic calculator program where the user can choose between addition, subtraction, multiplication, or division. Use a lambda expression to pass the specific operation into a method that performs the calculation. The method should accept two integers and a lambda expression that defines the operation.

3. **Banking Application**. Build a basic banking application where the user can deposit, withdraw, or check their balance. Delegate the deposit, withdrawal, and balance checking to separate methods. Ensure the system handles insufficient funds properly by validating balance before a withdrawal.

4. **Applying Discounts**. Write a program that calculates the price of an item after applying a discount. The discount can vary based on the type of customer (e.g., student, senior citizen, or regular customer). Use a lambda expression to pass the discount logic into a method that calculates the final price. Write code to test your program using two different discount calculations of your choosing.

5. **Game Health System**. Implement a health system for a game where a player's health can be increased based on certain conditions. Use a lambda expression to calculate a health bonus and pass it into a method that updates the player's total health. The method should also ensure that health never exceeds a maximum value. Write code to test your program demonstrating that your lambda expression works as specified above.

6. **Product Price Calculator with Customizable Tax**. Write a program that calculates the final price of a product after applying a customizable tax logic. Use a lambda expression to pass in the tax calculation logic. Write code to test your program using two different tax calculations of your choosing.

"But all things should be done decently and in order."
1 Corinthians 14:40 (ESV)

CHAPTER 7

MANAGING COLLECTIONS OF DATA

Introduction

From the very beginning of the Bible, we see that God is a God of order. Genesis 1 gives us a picture of God's creative process, where He brings form and structure to what was formless. As He created the universe, He separated light from darkness, sky from land, and water from dry ground. He ordered the days of creation, forming the heavens and the earth in the first three days and filling them with life in the next three. In doing so, God demonstrates that order and structure are essential to life itself. Without that order, there would be chaos, but with it, we see a beautiful, functioning system where each part has its place and works together in harmony.

The Bible also repeatedly calls us to seek order and structure in our lives. For example, 1 Corinthians 14:40 (ESV) reminds us, "But all things should be done decently and in order." In context, this is an instruction given to the church, emphasizing the importance of orderly conduct in worship so that everyone may benefit. This principle of order can also be applied to our personal lives, guiding us toward intentionality and discipline.

In the same way that God designed the universe with order, we can follow this example to bring structure and purpose to the systems we create. Creation consists of distinct elements, each serving a unique purpose, which serves as a pattern for our designs. In programming, our code should be composed of organized components that work well together. When working with programs, we often deal with vast amounts of data, which can quickly become overwhelming if not properly organized. Without a clear structure, managing or making sense of this information becomes nearly impossible. Data structures like arrays and lists provide the means to bring order to this data.

Consider an array in programming like a set of labeled storage bins. It provides a fixed location for each piece of data, making it easy for us to access or modify the information when needed. The programmer determines how the items are arranged and how each slot is used. However, sometimes our data is more complex and requires more than just one level of organization. For instance, we may need to represent multiple dimensions, such as a table of information, which can be managed using multidimensional arrays.

By recognizing the shape and dimensions of the data, we can determine the best way to organize it. Once organized, the data becomes much easier to work with. Whether processing elements in a one-dimensional array or working with rows and columns in a two-dimensional array, applying order and structure helps us manage complexity efficiently.

Ultimately, using arrays and lists reflects our desire to model the intentional order that we see in God's creation. By doing so, we create programs that are not only functional but also elegant and efficient, just as God's creation is both functional and beautiful.

Step 1. Understand the Problem

As Alex continues to develop his game, he realizes that managing a growing number of resources will soon become cumbersome. Right now, the game allows players to collect resources, but there's no organized way to store or manage them beyond the immediate turn. Alex wants to introduce a system where the player can track all the resources they collect over time, so they can be used for crafting new resources. This system will help keep the game structured and organized as the player's inventory grows.

Arrays are a natural choice for implementing an inventory system for the game. Using an array to track inventory allows the player to track their resources, while ensuring that there is a defined limit to how much a player can carry. Alex feels that this limitation creates an added layer of strategy for the player, since players will need to decide when to gather more resources and when to use or discard items to make space for new ones.

In addition to managing resources, Alex also wants to give players the ability to craft new items using the resources they've collected. To accomplish this, he plans to introduce a crafting system, which will allow the player to arrange resources in a 3x3 grid to create specific items. For example, to craft a sword, the player might need to place wood and steel in specific positions on the grid. This will not only add depth to the game play but also give players more meaningful choices in how they use their resources.

However, Alex must carefully consider how to handle the crafting system. For each crafting recipe, he'll need to define which resources are required and in what arrangement. The system will need to check the grid after the player places their resources, comparing the arrangement to a list of predefined recipes. If the arrangement matches a valid recipe, the item will be crafted and added to the player's inventory, but only if there's space. If the recipe does not match, or if the player's inventory is full, they'll lose the item and any resources that were placed in the grid. This approach provides a further incentive for players to manage their inventory well.

Step 2. Plan the Solution

To achieve Alex's main goal of introducing an inventory system and a crafting system to his game, he begins by outlining the key steps needed to bring these features to life.

Arrays

Before getting into implementing an inventory system, let's first understand what arrays are at a conceptual level. An **array** is a data structure that contains a sequence of values, all of which must be of the same variable type. Arrays have a predefined length, which means that initially, you specify how many elements the array will hold. Although it is possible to resize an array, doing so can be inefficient because it requires creating a new array and copying over the existing values. Therefore, it's usually best to choose an appropriate size for the array from the start.

Arrays are useful because they allow us to efficiently store and access multiple values with minimal effort. By giving each element in the array a specific position, we can easily retrieve, update, or iterate over the data. Whether it's keeping track of player stats or managing game resources, arrays offer a simple yet powerful way to handle collections of information.

In C#, arrays can be used to store both value types (like `int` or `float`) and reference types (like objects). When we create an array of a value type, each element in the array is automatically initialized with the default value for that type. For example, an `int` array will be filled with zeros and a `char` array will be filled with null characters (`'\0'`). When we create an array of a reference type, each element is initialized to `null` until we explicitly assign a value.

Let's walk through a simple example. Suppose we have a scenario where we want to keep track of the scores for five players in a game. Code Block 7.1 shows how we can use an array to store and retrieve these scores.

Code Block 7.1: Example One–Dimensional Array

```
1 | // Creating and initializing an array of integers
2 | int[] playerScores = new int[5];
3 |
4 | // Setting values for each player
5 | playerScores[0] = 10;
6 | playerScores[1] = 15;
7 | playerScores[2] = 20;
8 | playerScores[3] = 25;
9 | playerScores[4] = 30;
10 |
11 | // Retrieving values from the array
12 | Console.WriteLine($"Score of Player 1: {playerScores[0]}");
13 | Console.WriteLine($"Score of Player 2: {playerScores[1]}");
```

In this example, we first create an array called playerScores with five elements in line 2. By default, since int is a value type, all elements are initially set to 0. We then set each player's score individually (lines 5 through 9) and print out the values in lines 12 and 13.

Inventory Management

Now, let's move on to planning the inventory system for Alex's game. The first task is to implement a system that tracks all the resources the player collects. Since arrays have a fixed size, Alex decides to use an array to represent the player's inventory, setting an upper limit on how many types of resources the player can store at any given time. This introduces an element of scarcity management, so that once the inventory is full, the player must make decisions about what to keep and what to discard.

Alex knows that the array will need to hold objects that represent each type of resource. Each element in the array will represent a unique resource the player has collected. If the player collects more of a resource that they already have in inventory, the game should search through the array, find the matching resource object, and increase the amount of the resource accordingly. If the resource is new, it will be added to the first available empty spot in the array.

However, if the inventory is full, Alex wants to make sure that no new resources can be collected. In this case, the game will notify the player that their inventory is full, and they won't be able to collect any more resources until they free up space by crafting or discarding items. Alex creates the pseudo-code in Text Box 7.1 to describe the process for adding resources to the player's inventory.

Text Box 7.1: Pseudo-code for Adding Resources to Inventory

Set resource added equal to false
For each slot in the inventory:
    If the slot is empty:
        Add the resource to the empty slot.
        Mark resource added as true.
        Stop checking further.
    Else if the type of resource in the slot matches the type of resource being added:
        Increase the amount of that resource in inventory.
        Mark resource added as true.
        Stop checking further.
If resource added is still false:
    Notify the player that the inventory is full, and no resources can be collected.

This approach ensures that the inventory management system stays simple but effective, using the array to store up to a predefined number of resources and checking for available space each time a new resource is collected.

Two-Dimensional Arrays

Before we introduce the crafting system, let's first take a moment to understand what a two-dimensional array is. While a one-dimensional array is like a simple list that holds a sequence of values, a two-dimensional array is more like a grid or a table. It is an array of arrays, meaning that it has both rows and columns, which makes it useful for representing data that has two dimensions, like a checkerboard or a spreadsheet. In a two-dimensional array, you can access each element by specifying both its row and column index.

Let's consider a simple example where we want to represent a 3x3 tic-tac-toe board. In Code Block 7.2, we create a two-dimensional array named `ticTacToeBoard` with three rows and three columns in line 2. Initially, since char is a value type, all elements are set to the default value (`'\0'` or the null character). We use a nested `for` loop (lines 5 through 11) to set each cell to a space character (`' '`) to make it easier to visualize an empty board. We then set specific cells to represent players' moves (lines 14 and 15) and print out the values to verify them (lines 18 and 19).

Code Block 7.2: Example Two–Dimensional Array

```csharp
1  // Creating and initializing a two-dimensional array
2  char[,] ticTacToeBoard = new char[3, 3];
3
4  // Initializing the board with empty spaces
5  for (int row = 0; row < 3; row++)
6  {
7      for (int column = 0; column < 3; column++)
8      {
9          ticTacToeBoard[row, column] = ' ';
10     }
11 }
12
13 // Setting some values on the board
14 ticTacToeBoard[0, 0] = 'X';
15 ticTacToeBoard[1, 1] = 'O';
16
17 // Retrieving values from the board
18 Console.WriteLine($"Top-left cell: {ticTacToeBoard[0, 0]}");
19 Console.WriteLine($"Center cell: {ticTacToeBoard[1, 1]}");
```

Crafting System

Alex moves on to planning the crafting system. Players will be able to use the resources they collect to craft new items. The crafting system will feature a 3x3 grid, represented by a two-dimensional array. Players will place resources in specific slots on the grid, and the system will compare this arrangement to predefined recipes to determine whether a valid item can be crafted.

Each recipe will be stored in a Recipe class, which defines the arrangement of resources required to craft an item. For example, to craft a sword, the recipe might require steel in the top-middle and center squares and wood in the bottom-middle square on the grid. If the player places the correct resources in the correct positions, the recipe will match, and the item can be crafted.

Checking for a valid recipe will involve comparing the resources placed on the crafting grid with the resources in each recipe within the crafting system. To do this, Alex will need to loop through the recipes in the crafting system and compare the recipe's pattern with the items that the player has placed on the crafting grid. Alex uses the Expert Pattern to delegate the responsibility for matching the crafting grid with a single recipe to the `Recipe` class. He designs the pseudo-code for this process in Text Box 7.2. This approach allows Alex to keep the crafting system simple while providing flexibility to add more recipes in the future.

Text Box 7.2: Pseudo-code for Matches Method

For each row in the grid provided:
    For each column in that row:
        If the resource at that row and column does not match the recipe's resource:
            Return false indicating the recipe does not match
Return true to indicate the given recipe matches

Crafting Items

Players will place resources into the 3x3 crafting grid by selecting which resources from their inventory they want to use and where they want to place them on the grid. Once they are satisfied with the arrangement, they will attempt to craft an item. The crafting system will then use the method described earlier to see if the items on the grid match a valid recipe. If the arrangement matches a valid recipe, the crafted item will be added to their inventory (assuming there's space); otherwise, the resources on the grid will be lost. Alex creates the pseudo-code in Text Box 7.3 to model the crafting process.

Finally, Alex needs to ensure that the crafting system and inventory system work well together. The plan for these mechanics emphasizes the use of arrays to store and manage collections of data. The single-dimension array in the inventory system allows Alex to manage the player's resources, while the two-dimensional array in the crafting system allows for flexible arrangements of resources to create new resources. Arrays are a powerful way to organize data in C#. Whether using a simple one-dimensional array or a more complex two-dimensional array, they provide structure that makes managing and accessing data more efficient.

To finish his plan for the solution, Alex prepares the class diagram in Figure 7.1 with all the new classes and methods he will need to accomplish his pseudo-code. This visual representation helps Alex confirm that all the necessary components are accounted for and clearly defined. With a solid plan in place, Alex is now ready to implement these systems, ensuring that the game's new mechanics are well-structured and easy to manage.

Text Box 7.3: Pseudo-code for Crafting Items

While the player wants to craft:
    Display the player's inventory.
    Display the crafting grid.
    Display options to add resource, remove resource, craft, or cancel crafting
    If the player wants to add a resource:
        Ask the player for grid location
        Ask the player to select a resource to place on the crafting grid.
        If the selected resource has more than 0 amount left:
            Place the resource in the chosen slot.
            Remove 1 resource from the player's inventory.
        Else:
            Notify the player that they do not have enough of that resource.
    Else if the player wants to remove a resource:
        Ask player to choose a slot from the crafting grid to remove the resource.
        Set the chosen slot to None
    Else if the player wants to attempt crafting:
        Check the crafting grid against predefined recipes.
        If the grid matches a recipe:
            Craft the item.
            If there is room in the player's inventory:
                Add the item to the player's inventory.
            Else:
                Notify player that their inventory is full, and crafted item is lost.
            Clear the crafting grid.
        Otherwise:
            Notify the player that no valid recipe was found.
            Clear the crafting grid (all resources in the grid are lost).
    Else if the player wants to cancel crafting:
        Set crafting status to false

Step 3. Implement the Solution

With a clear plan in place, Alex begins implementing the new mechanics for the game. The first task is to add an inventory system for managing collected resources. Then, he will implement the crafting system that allows players to craft items from their inventory, using the crafting grid. Finally, he will update the game's menu to support these new features.

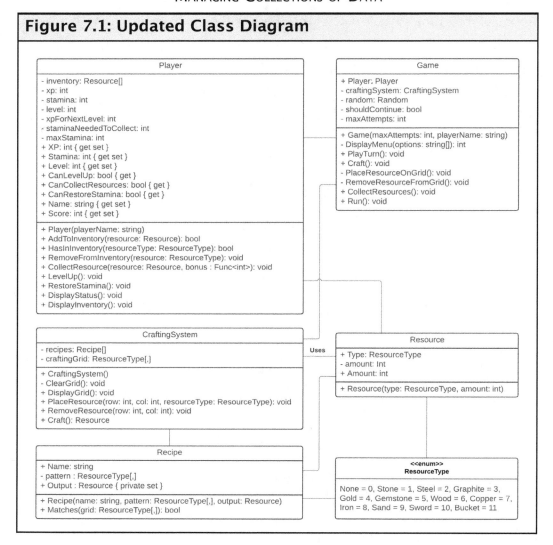

Figure 7.1: Updated Class Diagram

Implementing the Inventory System

Alex starts by updating the Player class, as shown in Code Block 7.3, to include an array for storing the player's inventory of resources. The array will hold a maximum of 10 Resource objects. When the player collects a new resource, the game will first check whether that resource type already exists in the inventory. If it does, the existing amount will be incremented. If the resource is not yet in the inventory, it will be added to the next available slot. If there are no available slots, meaning the inventory is full, the player is informed that they cannot collect any more resources. This design ensures efficient item stacking and prevents inventory overflow.

Code Block 7.3: Updated Player Class

```
 1| public class Player
 2| {
 3|
 4|   private Resource[] inventory;
 5|
 6|   // Other Player properties here...
 7|
 8|   public Player(string name)
 9|   {
10|     inventory = new Resource[10];    // Can store up to 10 resources.
11|     // Other constructor statements here...
12|   }
13|
14|
15|   public bool AddToInventory(Resource resource)
16|   {
17|     bool resourceAdded = false;
18|     for (int index = 0; index < inventory.Length; index++)
19|     {
20|       if (inventory[index] == null)
21|       {
22|         inventory[index] = resource;
23|         resourceAdded = true;
24|         break;
25|       }
26|       else if (inventory[index].Type == resource.Type)
27|       {
28|         inventory[index].Amount += resource.Amount;
29|         resourceAdded = true;
30|         break;
31|       }
32|     }
33|     return resourceAdded;
34|   }
35|
36|
37|   public void CollectResource(Resource resource, Func<int> bonus)
38|   {
39|     if (CanCollectResources)
40|     {
41|       if (AddToInventory(resource))
42|       {
43|         switch (resource.Amount)
44|         {
45|           // Bonus calculation case statements here...
46|         }
47|         Stamina -= staminaNeededToCollect;
48|       }
49|       else
50|       {
51|         Console.WriteLine($"Inventory is full!");
52|       }
53|     }
54|     else
55|     {
56|       Console.WriteLine("Not enough stamina to collect resources!");
57|     }
58|   }
59|
60|
61|
```

(continued on next page) →

```
62|  → (continued from previous page)
63|
64|    public bool RemoveFromInventory(Resource resource)
65|    {
66|      for (int index = 0; index < inventory.Length; index++)
67|      {
68|        if (inventory[index] != null && inventory[index].Type == resource.Type)
69|        {
70|          if (inventory[index].Amount >= resource.Amount)
71|          {
72|            inventory[index].Amount -= resource.Amount;
73|
74|            // If the amount goes to zero, remove the resource from the inventory
75|            if (inventory[index].Amount == 0)
76|            {
77|              inventory[index] = null;
78|            }
79|            Console.WriteLine($"{resource.Amount} {resource.Type} removed from
                 your inventory.");
80|            return true;
81|          }
82|          else
83|          {
84|            Console.WriteLine($"Not enough {resource.Type} to remove.");
85|            return false;
86|          }
87|        }
88|      }
89|
90|    public bool HasInInventory(ResourceType resourceType)
91|    {
92|      for (int index = 0; index < inventory.Length; index++)
93|      {
94|        if (inventory[index] != null && inventory[index].Type == resourceType)
95|        {
96|          return true;
97|        }
98|      }
99|      return false;
100|   }
101|
102|   public void DisplayInventory()
103|   {
104|     Console.WriteLine("Inventory:");
105|     // Loop through each item in the inventory array
106|     for (int index = 0; index < inventory.Length; index++)
107|     {
108|       if (inventory[index] != null)
109|       {
110|         // Display details of the item if it's not null
111|         Console.WriteLine($"Slot {index + 1}:");
112|         Console.WriteLine($" - Type: {inventory[index].Type}");
113|         Console.WriteLine($" - Amount: {inventory[index].Amount}");
114|       }
115|     }
116|     Console.WriteLine(); // Add a blank line for better readability
117|   }
118|   // Other player methods here...
119| }
```

When Alex was planning the inventory system, he recognized that the logic for adding items to the player's inventory would be used frequently throughout the game. The player will often add resources they collect, as well as crafted items, making the need for a consistent approach clear. Alex ensures that all inventory-related additions follow the same rules by centralizing this logic in the AddToInventory method. This change reduces redundancy and makes future modifications easier since any changes to how items are added can now be made in a single location.

In addition to adding items, Alex realizes that the player will also need to remove resources from inventory, especially during crafting. To manage this, he adds a RemoveFromInventory method, which ensures that resources are properly reduced when they are used, and removes an item entirely if its amount reaches zero. Similarly, Alex adds a HasInInventory method to check whether the player possesses a specific resource type, which is particularly helpful during crafting when checking for required materials.

The AddToInventory method handles the addition of resources by first trying to stack similar resources and only adding new items if there is space available. If the inventory is full, a message informs the player. The CollectResource method then calls AddToInventory, making it more focused and easier to understand. The RemoveFromInventory method, on the other hand, ensures that resources are removed cleanly, while HasInInventory allows the game to check if a specific resource type exists in the inventory. Finally, the DisplayInventory method keeps the player informed of their current resource status in an organized manner.

This refactored approach centralizes inventory management, ensuring consistency in how items are added and removed, enforcing inventory limits, and efficiently managing the resources. By separating the task of inventory management into dedicated methods, Alex makes the code more flexible, reusable, and easier to maintain.

Implementing the Crafting System

The crafting system is the next step in the implementation process. To support crafting, Alex needs to define specific recipes. A Recipe class is used to store the pattern of resources required for crafting an item. Each recipe has a name (such as "Steel Sword" or "Wood Shovel") and a 3x3 array that defines the arrangement of resources needed to craft the item. Code Block 7.4 shows how the Recipe class is structured.

Code Block 7.4: Recipe Class

```
1  public class Recipe
2  {
3     public string Name { get; set; }
4     private ResourceType[,] pattern;
5     public Resource Result { get; private set; }
6
7     public Recipe(string name, ResourceType[,] pattern, Resource result)
8     {
9        Name = name;
10       this.pattern = pattern;
11       Result = result;
12    }
13
14    // Method to check if the current grid matches the recipe pattern
15    public bool Matches(ResourceType[,] grid)
16    {
17       for (int row = 0; row < 3; row++)
18       {
19          for (int column = 0; column < 3; column++)
20          {
21             if (grid[row, column] != pattern[row, column])
22             {
23                return false;  // If any cell doesn't match, the recipe fails
24             }
25          }
26       }
27       return true;  // If all cells match, the recipe is valid
28    }
29 }
```

The Recipe class contains the Name and a 3x3 Pattern array of ResourceType that defines the recipe. The Matches method compares the player's current crafting grid to the recipe pattern, checking whether each resource in the grid matches the expected resource in the recipe.

To manage crafting, Alex creates a CraftingSystem class. This class contains a 3x3 grid represented by a two-dimensional array of ResourceType. Alex soon realizes that not all recipes will require a resource in every square of the grid, but since the ResourceType enumeration is a value type, the grid array cannot hold null values to indicate an empty cell. To solve this, Alex inserts an enumeration value called None at the beginning of the enumeration to represent an empty slot on the grid, along with some additional resource types at the end.

To craft an item, the player places resources on the grid, and the system compares the grid's contents to predefined recipes. If the grid matches a valid recipe, the item is crafted. Code Block 7.5 shows how the `CraftingSystem` class is implemented.

Code Block 7.5: CraftingSystem Class

```
 1| public enum ResourceType
 2| {
 3|    None = 0, Stone = 1, Steel = 2, Graphite = 3, Gold = 4, Gemstone = 5,
 4|    Wood = 6, Copper = 7, Iron = 8, Sand = 9, Sword = 10, Bucket = 11
 5| }
 6|
 7| public class CraftingSystem
 8| {
 9|    private Recipe[] recipes = new Recipe[5]; // Store available recipes
10|    private ResourceType[,] craftingGrid = new ResourceType[3, 3]; // 3x3 Grid
11|
12|    public CraftingSystem()
13|    {
14|       ClearGrid(); // Initialize the crafting grid to be empty (None)
15|       // Example recipe for a steel sword
16|       recipes[0] = new Recipe("Steel Sword", new ResourceType[,]
17|          {
18|             { ResourceType.None, ResourceType.Steel, ResourceType.None },
19|             { ResourceType.None, ResourceType.Steel, ResourceType.None },
20|             { ResourceType.None, ResourceType.Wood, ResourceType.None }
21|          },
22|          new Resource(ResourceType.Sword, 1)
23|       );
24|       // Add more recipes here...
25|    }
26|
27|    // Method to remove all resources from the grid
28|    public void ClearGrid()
29|    {
30|       for (int row = 0; row < 3; row++)
31|       {
32|          for (int column = 0; column < 3; column++)
33|          {
34|             craftingGrid[row, column] = ResourceType.None;
35|          }
36|       }
37|    }
38|
39|    // Method to place a resource on the grid
40|    public void PlaceResource(int row, int col, ResourceType type)
41|    {
42|       craftingGrid[row, col] = type;
43|
44|       Console.WriteLine($"Placed {type} at position ({row}, {col})");
45|    }
46|
47|    // Method to remove resource from the grid
48|    public void RemoveResource(int row, int column)
49|    {
50|       craftingGrid[row, column] = ResourceType.None;
51|    }
52|
```

(continued on next page) →

```
53|  → (continued from previous page)
54|
55|    // Method to attempt crafting
56|    public Resource Craft()
57|    {
58|      foreach (var recipe in recipes)
59|      {
60|        if (recipe != null && recipe.Matches(craftingGrid))
61|        {
62|          Console.WriteLine($"Crafted {recipe.Name}!");
63|          return recipe.Result;
64|        }
65|      }
66|      Console.WriteLine("No matching recipe found.");
67|      return null;
68|    }
69|  }
```

The crafting grid is represented as a 3x3 array of ResourceType, initially filled with ResourceType.None to indicate empty slots. The PlaceResource method allows the player to place a resource in a specific grid slot. The RemoveResource method allows the player to remove the resource from the specified grid slot at the cost of losing the resource. The Craft method checks if the current grid layout matches any of the available recipes, and if a match is found, the corresponding item is crafted, and a message is displayed. This ensures that crafting always requires the correct resources in the right pattern. Let's take a closer look at the foreach loop that Alex used in the Craft method.

Introducing the foreach Loop

As Alex developed the Craft method he faced the challenge of checking whether the player's current crafting grid matched any of the available recipes. To solve this problem efficiently, he decided to use a foreach loop, a tool that made it easy to iterate over each recipe in his collection.

Unlike the for loops Alex used earlier in the book, which required him to manually manage loop counters and indices, the foreach loop allows him to move through every recipe without needing to worry about how many recipes there were or keeping track of their positions in the list. The simplicity of the foreach loop means Alex can focus directly on the task of comparing each recipe, making his code both cleaner and easier to understand.

The syntax of the `foreach` loop is shown in Code Block 7.6. The `var` keyword represents the data type of each element in the collection, allowing C# to automatically determine the type based on the context. Alternatively, you can explicitly specify the type, but using `var` often makes the code more concise and readable. The variable that follows, such as element, holds the current item from the collection during each iteration, allowing you to work with that item directly. Finally, the collection itself can be an array, a list, or any other enumerable collection that you want to iterate over. The loop will move through each element in the collection, executing the code inside the loop block for every item it encounters.

Code Block 7.6: Syntax of the `foreach` Loop

```
1| foreach (var element in collection)
2| {
3|    // Code to execute for each element
4| }
```

In Code Block 7.5, Alex used the `foreach` loop in lines 58 through 65 to go through each recipe in the recipes array. For each recipe, he first made sure it wasn't `null` and then asked the recipe if it matched the resources currently placed on the crafting grid. If the recipe matched, the item is crafted, and the player is notified of the result. If no match was found after going through all the recipes, a message informs the player that their current arrangement isn't valid for crafting.

The `foreach` loop is perfect for this scenario. It allows Alex to seamlessly iterate over the available recipes without worrying about how to manage indices or access each element in the array. However, as he works with the `foreach` loop, Alex also realizes an important limitation; it is not possible to modify the collection while iterating through it. This means that he cannot add or remove recipes during the iteration. If the crafting system had required recipes to be dynamically added or removed, he would need to use a different approach, such as a `for` loop or creating a separate collection to modify. Despite this limitation, the `foreach` loop proves effective for Alex's purposes with the crafting process.

Updating the Game Class

After implementing the initial crafting and inventory features, Alex realizes that he can refine the way the player interacts with the game's menu. He wants the game menu to be easy to update, especially since the addition of crafting has introduced several new options. With future features potentially on the horizon, Alex decides it is essential to refactor the way the menu system works.

Refactoring the Game Menu

Instead of having repetitive code for displaying menus in different parts of the game, Alex identifies an opportunity for optimization. He notices that the logic for displaying menus and validating user choices is similar whether the player is choosing a main action, interacting with the crafting grid, or selecting from a list of available resources. Refactoring this logic into a single method that handles menu options makes his code more concise and easier to maintain.

Code Block 7.7: The DisplayMenu Method

```
 1 | private int DisplayMenu(string[] options)
 2 | {
 3 |   int choice;
 4 |   do
 5 |   {
 6 |     Console.WriteLine("Choose an action: ");
 7 |     for (int index = 0; index < options.Length; index++)
 8 |     {
 9 |       Console.WriteLine($"{index + 1}. {options[index]}");
10 |     }
11 |     string input = Console.ReadLine();
12 |     bool isValid = int.TryParse(input, out choice);
13 |     if (!isValid || choice < 1 || choice > options.Length)
14 |     {
15 |       Console.WriteLine($"Enter a number between 1 and {options.Length}.");
16 |     }
17 |   } while (choice < 1 || choice > options.Length);
18 |   return choice;
19 | }
```

With this in mind, Alex alters the DisplayMenu method to accept an array of strings representing menu options and returns the player's choice. The DisplayMenu method, as shown in Code Block 7.7, handles displaying the available options, validating the player's input, and repeating the prompt until a valid selection is made.

Alex then updates the PlayTurn method, as shown in Code Block 7.8, to use the new DisplayMenu method for presenting the main game menu. The PlayTurn method calls DisplayMenu with the list of available actions, waits for the player's choice, and then invokes the corresponding game functionality. For example, if the player chooses to craft an item, the Craft method is called to enter crafting mode. In crafting mode, the player has further options, such as placing or removing resources on the crafting grid or attempting to craft an item.

Code Block 7.8: The PlayTurn Method

```
 1 | public void PlayTurn()
 2 | {
 3 |    // Show player's status before each action
 4 |    Player.DisplayStatus();
 5 |    string[] options = { "Collect Resources", "Restore Stamina", "Level Up",
    ↳    "Show Inventory", "Craft", "Quit" };
 6 |    int choice = DisplayMenu(options);
 7 |    switch (choice)
 8 |    {
 9 |      case 1:
10 |        CollectResources();
11 |        break;
12 |      case 2:
13 |        Player.RestoreStamina();
14 |        break;
15 |      case 3:
16 |        Player.LevelUp();
17 |        break;
18 |      case 4:
19 |        Player.DisplayInventory();
20 |        break;
21 |      case 5:
22 |        Craft();
23 |        break;
24 |      case 6:
25 |        Console.WriteLine("Thanks for playing!");
26 |        shouldContinue = false;
27 |        break;
28 |    }
29 | }
```

Introducing Crafting Mode

Alex incorporates the newly designed DisplayMenu method within the crafting system as well, as shown in Code Block 7.9. When the player chooses to craft from the main menu, the Craft method is called, where the code enters a loop that continues until crafting is complete or the player chooses to exit crafting mode. Each time through the loop, Alex uses the DisplayMenu method to let the player choose their crafting action, such as placing a resource on the grid, removing a resource, attempting to craft, or canceling the crafting session. For example, when placing a resource on the grid, the player is prompted to select the grid row and column as well as the resource type. This refactored crafting interaction is not only more intuitive for the player, but also much cleaner in the code.

Code Block 7.9: Updated Crafting Process in Game Class

```
1| public void Craft()
2| {
3|    Console.WriteLine("Entering crafting mode...");
4|    bool crafting = true;
5|    while (crafting)
6|    {
7|       Player.DisplayInventory();
8|       Console.WriteLine("Crafting Grid:");
9|       craftingSystem.DisplayGrid();
10|      string[] options = { "Place a resource on the grid",
        "Remove a resource from the grid", "Attempt to craft",
        "Cancel crafting" };
11|      int choice = DisplayMenu(options);
12|      switch (choice)
13|      {
14|         case 1:
15|            PlaceResourceOnGrid();
16|            break;
17|         case 2:
18|            RemoveResourceFromGrid();
19|            break;
20|         case 3:
21|            var craftedItem = craftingSystem.Craft();
22|            if (craftedItem != null)
23|            {
24|               Player.AddToInventory(craftedItem);
25|               Console.WriteLine($"Successfully crafted: {craftedItem.Type}");
26|               crafting = false; // Exit crafting loop after successful crafting
27|            }
28|            else
29|            {
30|               Console.WriteLine("No matching recipe found. Try again.");
31|            }
32|            break;
33|         case 4:
34|            Console.WriteLine("Exiting crafting mode.");
35|            crafting = false;
36|            break;
37|      }
38|   }
39| }
40|
41| // Helper method to place a resource on the crafting grid
42| private void PlaceResourceOnGrid()
43| {
44|    string[] rows = { "Top Row", "Middle Row", "Bottom Row" };
45|    int row = DisplayMenu(rows) - 1;
46|                                        (continued on next page) →
```

```
47|  → (continued from previous page)
48|
49|     string[] columns = { "Left Column", "Middle Column", "Right Column" };
50|     int column = DisplayMenu(columns) - 1;
51|
52|     string[] resources = Enum.GetNames(typeof(ResourceType));
53|     int resourceIndex = DisplayMenu(resources) - 1;
54|     ResourceType resourceType = (ResourceType)resourceIndex;
55|
56|
57|     if (Player.HasInInventory(resourceType))
58|     {
59|         craftingSystem.PlaceResource(row, column, resourceType);
60|         Console.WriteLine($"{resourceType} placed at ({row}, {column}).");
61|         // Remove one unit of the resource from inventory
62|         Player.RemoveFromInventory(resourceType, 1);
63|     }
64|     else
65|     {
66|         Console.WriteLine($"There is no {resourceType} in your inventory.");
67|     }
68| }
69|
70| // Helper method to remove a resource from the crafting grid
71| private void RemoveResourceFromGrid()
72| {
73|     string[] rows = { "Top Row", "Middle Row", "Bottom Row" };
74|     int row = DisplayMenu(rows) - 1;
75|
76|     string[] columns = { "Left Column", "Middle Column", "Right Column" };
77|     int column = DisplayMenu(columns) - 1;
78|
79|     craftingSystem.RemoveResource(row, column);
80| }
```

Streamlining the Crafting System Integration

When the player attempts to craft an item using the crafting grid, the
CraftingSystem is responsible for determining whether the recipe
matches the grid's current configuration. Though it's not shown in the
code block, Alex adds a field to the Game class called craftingSystem,
which is an instance of the CraftingSystem class. This instance is used
to access the crafting grid, manage resource placements, and validate
recipes during the crafting process. If a match is found, the resulting item
is returned to the Game class, which then passes it to the player's inventory
through the AddToInventory method. This decoupled design ensures
that each class focuses on its intended responsibilities, resulting in more
maintainable and scalable code.

Alex also includes utility methods for interacting with the crafting
grid, such as placing and removing resources. These methods guide

the player through the crafting process while ensuring that resource quantities are accurately tracked.

The crafting experience is now dynamic and allows for more complex interactions. Players can choose which resources to place, determine the configuration on the crafting grid, and ultimately craft new items that contribute to their progress in the game. With this refactor, Alex sets up the foundation for adding more advanced features to the game while keeping the code clean, manageable, and easy to extend.

Step 4. Test the Solution

Now that Alex has implemented the new inventory and crafting systems, he moves on to testing his solution. His goal is to ensure that the player can seamlessly interact with the game's features: collecting resources, managing their inventory, crafting items, and selecting actions from the menu.

Testing the Inventory System

To begin, Alex focuses on testing the inventory system, ensuring that players can store resources in their inventory, and update existing resources when additional quantities of the same type are collected. Additionally, Alex needs to confirm that the game properly prevents further collection when the inventory reaches full capacity.

Alex begins by testing the AddToInventory method to ensure that it correctly adds resources to the inventory or updates the amount of an existing resource. He uses the DisplayInventory method to help him evaluate the results of his test, effectively testing two methods at once. The test begins by creating a player instance, and then three resource objects, two of which are wood, as shown in Code Block 7.10. He adds the resources to the player's inventory, and then displays the player's resulting inventory. Alex expects the player's inventory to show 25 units of wood and 5 units of steel, verifying that the resources stack correctly and amounts update as intended.

Code Block 7.10: Inventory Add Test

```
 1| Player player = new("Alex");
 2|
 3| // Simulate collecting 10 units of wood
 4| Resource wood = new(ResourceType.Wood, 10);
 5| player.AddToInventory(wood);
 6|
 7| // Simulate collecting 5 units of steel
 8| Resource steel = new(ResourceType.Steel, 5);
 9| player.AddToInventory(steel);
10|
11| // Simulate collecting another 15 units of wood
12| Resource moreWood = new(ResourceType.Wood, 15);
13| player.AddToInventory(moreWood);
14|
15| player.DisplayInventory();
```

Next, Alex tests the removal of resources to confirm that resources can be appropriately depleted from the inventory, as shown in Code Block 7.11. Using the RemoveFromInventory method, he removes specific quantities of a resource to validate that the resource amounts update correctly and that resources are removed from the inventory entirely when their quantity reaches zero. This also verifies the message output when the player attempts to remove more of a resource than is available in inventory.

Code Block 7.11: Inventory Remove Test

```
 1| Player player = new("Alex");
 2| Resource wood = new(ResourceType.Wood, 10);
 3| player.AddToInventory(wood);
 4|
 5| // Check if the player has wood in the inventory (should be true)
 6| Console.WriteLine($"Has wood in inventory: {player.
  ↪   HasInInventory(ResourceType.Wood)}");
 7|
 8| // Remove 6 units of wood from the inventory
 9| Resource woodToRemove = new(ResourceType.Wood, 6);
10| player.RemoveFromInventory(woodToRemove);
11|
12| // Display the player's inventory to check updated quantity
13| player.DisplayInventory();
14|
15| // Attempt to remove another 6 units of wood from the inventory; should fail
16| player.RemoveFromInventory(woodToRemove);
17|
18| // Remove the remaining units of wood from the inventory
19| woodToRemove.Amount = 4;
20| player.RemoveFromInventory(woodToRemove);
21|
22| // Check if the player still has wood in the inventory (should be true)
23| Console.WriteLine($"Has wood in inventory: {player.
  ↪   HasInInventory(ResourceType.Wood)}");
```

Next, Alex tests what happens when the inventory is full. Since the `Inventory` array has a fixed size, attempting to collect additional resources after the inventory is full should return false indicating that the player can't carry any more, as shown in Code Block 7.12. In this case, Alex expects the game to display the message "Added? True" 10 times (once for each time through the loop on line 9), followed by "Added? False" when the code tries to add the bucket in line 16.

Code Block 7.12: Inventory Full Test

```
 1| Player player = new("Alex");
 2|
 3| // Fill all 10 inventory inventory slots with resources
 4| for (int i = 0; i < 10; i++)
 5| {
 6|    // Start from 1 to skip ResourceType.None
 7|    ResourceType resourceType = (ResourceType)(i + 1);
 8|    Resource resource = new(resourceType, 5);
 9|    Console.WriteLine($"Added? {player.AddToInventory(resource)}");
10| }
11|
12| // Attempt to collect a different resource when inventory is full
13| Resource bucket = new(ResourceType.Bucket, 3);
14|
15| // This should print Added? false
16| Console.WriteLine($"Added? {player.AddToInventory(bucket)}");
```

Testing the Crafting System

With the inventory system working, Alex moves on to testing the crafting system. In the game, the player can place resources on a 3x3 crafting grid to craft specific items based on predefined recipes. The `CraftingSystem` class manages the crafting process, checking the grid's configuration and matching it against the available recipes.

To test this system, Alex starts by attempting to craft a sword. The recipe for a sword requires steel in the top-middle and center positions of the grid, with wood in the bottom-middle position. Alex sets up the crafting grid and places these resources accordingly, as shown in Code Block 7.13. After placing the resources, Alex expects the `CraftingSystem` to identify that this matches the recipe for a sword and successfully craft the sword, and return it. The test then displays the type of the crafted resource. Alex expects the test to display, "Crafted resource: Sword."

Code Block 7.13: Crafting System Test with Matching Recipe

```
 1| // Set up the crafting system
 2| CraftingSystem craftingSystem = new();
 3|
 4| // Place steel in the top-middle and center positions
 5| craftingSystem.PlaceResource(0, 1, ResourceType.Steel);
 6| craftingSystem.PlaceResource(1, 1, ResourceType.Steel);
 7|
 8| // Place wood in the bottom-middle position
 9| craftingSystem.PlaceResource(1, 1, ResourceType.Wood);
10|
11| // Attempt to craft an item based on the grid
12| Resource craftedResource = craftingSystem.Craft();
13| if (craftedResource != null)
14| {
15|   Console.WriteLine($"Crafted resource: {craftedResource.Type}");
16| }
17| else
18| {
19|   Console.WriteLine("No resource crafted!");
20| }
```

Next, Alex tests what happens when the grid doesn't match any valid recipe. He places random resources on the grid and tries to craft an item, as shown in Code Block 7.14.

Code Block 7.14: Crafting System Test with Invalid Recipe

```
 1| // Set up the crafting system
 2| CraftingSystem craftingSystem = new();
 3|
 4| // Set up the crafting grid with random resources
 5| craftingSystem.PlaceResource(0, 0, ResourceType.Graphite);
 6| craftingSystem.PlaceResource(1, 2, ResourceType.Stone);
 7| craftingSystem.PlaceResource(2, 0, ResourceType.Steel);
 8|
 9| // Attempt to craft an item with no valid recipe
10| Resource craftedResource = craftingSystem.Craft();
11| if (craftedResource != null)
12| {
13|   Console.WriteLine($"Crafted resource: {craftedResource.Type}");
14| }
15| else
16| {
17|   Console.WriteLine("No resource crafted!");
18| }
```

In this scenario, since no recipe matches the grid's configuration, Alex expects the game to display the message, "No matching recipe found." This confirms that the crafting system can correctly differentiate between valid and invalid crafting attempts.

Testing the Menu System

With both the inventory and crafting systems verified, Alex turns his attention to testing the game's updated menu system. Each turn, the player should be presented with a menu that allows them to choose between collecting resources, restoring stamina, leveling up, crafting items, or quitting the game.

Alex starts by testing the option to collect resources. When the player selects this option from the menu, the game should correctly initiate the resource collection process, updating the inventory accordingly. Next, Alex tests the crafting option to ensure that the crafting menu displays properly and guides the player through the crafting process. When the player chooses to craft from the main menu, the game should enter crafting mode and display the crafting options, including placing a resource on the grid, removing a resource, attempting to craft, and canceling crafting.

First, Alex tests placing a resource on the crafting grid. The game prompts the player to choose a row and column where the resource should be placed and then asks for the type of resource. Alex ensures that if the selected resource exists in the player's inventory, it is placed correctly on the crafting grid, and the inventory is updated to reflect the reduced quantity. If the player attempts to place a resource they do not have, the game should display an appropriate message indicating that they lack the required resource.

Next, Alex tests removing resources from the grid. After placing several resources on different parts of the grid, he selects the option to remove them. The game prompts the player to specify the row and column of the resource to be removed. Alex expects the game to clear the specified slot on the crafting grid and update the crafting grid display.

Finally, Alex tests the crafting process itself. After configuring the crafting grid with the correct combination of resources, Alex selects the option to attempt crafting. The game checks if the resources match any available recipe. If a match is found, the game should craft the item and add it to the player's inventory, while also clearing the crafting grid. If no recipe matches the current configuration, the game should inform the player that no valid recipe was found and allow them to continue modifying the grid. Alex ensures that both successful and failed crafting attempts work as expected, making the crafting experience engaging and consistent for the player.

Additionally, Alex tests the "Show Inventory" option to ensure that the inventory contents are displayed accurately. He verifies that the inventory reflects all recent changes, such as resource collection, crafting additions, and item removal, providing the player with a clear and up-to-date view of their current items.

Even though Alex has already tested the features related to restoring stamina, leveling up, and quitting the game, he decides to test each menu option again to ensure that recent changes haven't introduced any new issues. He starts by testing the "Restore Stamina" option, where the game should deduct XP and increase the player's stamina appropriately. He then tests the "Level Up" option to confirm its correct functionality. Lastly, Alex tests the "Quit" option to ensure that the game exits gracefully when the player chooses to stop playing.

By systematically testing each feature of the game, Alex ensures that the new game play mechanics work seamlessly together. The inventory system properly tracks collected resources, prevents overfilling, and updates existing resources correctly. The crafting system matches recipes based on the player's input and provides clear feedback when items are crafted or when no valid recipe is found. Finally, the menu system allows players to make important decisions each turn and interact with the game's mechanics without any issues.

Step 5. Refine and Optimize

After thoroughly testing the game's mechanics, Alex noticed some limitations in how the player's inventory is managed. Specifically, using a fixed-size array for the inventory presented some challenges. While the array worked, it required predefining a maximum size for the inventory, meaning that Alex had to decide up front how many different types of resources the player could collect. In addition, the unused slots had to be filled with placeholder values, which often led to "None" resources cluttering the inventory. Though this system was functional, it felt clunky and cumbersome. Alex began to wonder if there was a more flexible and efficient way to manage the player's inventory.

The Generic List

After considering different approaches, Alex decides to refine the inventory system by replacing the array with a List<T>, a more dynamic data structure that can grow and shrink as needed. Unlike arrays, lists do not require setting a fixed size, nor do they need placeholder values for empty slots. The List<T> can expand or contract as resources are added or removed, making it an ideal solution for the game, since inventory frequently changes.

Before we get into the new inventory system, it is important to understand how a List<T> works in C#. Creating a List<T> involves using angle brackets to specify the type of elements the list will hold. For example, if Alex wants to create a list to hold resources in the player's inventory, he will write something like the code shown in Code Block 7.15. In line 1, Alex identifies that the code that follows will use a class in the System.Collections.Generic namespace. This namespace is where the List<T> class is defined. In line 2, List<Resource> means that this list will hold Resource objects, and the angle brackets (<>) are used to indicate the type of items the list can contain.

Code Block 7.15: Creating an Instance of a Generic List

```
1| using System.Collections.Generic;
2| List<Resource> playerInventory = new();
```

Once the list is created, adding items is straightforward. The List<T> class defines the Add() method to add items into the list. Alex can use the Add() method to add new resources, like wood or steel, to the player inventory. Unlike with arrays, there is no need to worry about exceeding a predefined size, as the list automatically resizes to accommodate any new items. Removing items is equally simple. If Alex decides that a particular resource, such as wood, is no longer needed, he can use the Remove() method to take it out of the inventory. Alternatively, if he wants to remove a specific item based on its position in the list, he can use RemoveAt(index) to remove an item at a given index.

Accessing items in a list is much like accessing elements in an array. Alex can use square brackets with an index to retrieve a particular item. For instance, to get the first item in the inventory, Alex could write inventory[0]. This allows easy access and update of the items in the list, as well as iterating over each element.

Modifying the `CollectResource` Method

With this understanding in place, Alex begins refining the inventory system by replacing the Resource[] array in the Player class with a List<Resource>. This change allows the inventory to expand dynamically, removing the need to handle None entries to represent unused inventory slots. Code Block 7.16 shows how Alex modifies the Player class.

Code Block 7.16: Updated Player Class with a List

```
1  using System;
2  using System.Collections.Generic;
3
4  public class Player
5  {
6      public List<Resource> Inventory { get; private set; }
7
8      // Other player properties here...
9
10     public Player(string playerName)
11     {
12         // List is now used instead of an array
13         Inventory = new List<Resource>();
14
15         // Other constructor statements here...
16     }
17
18     public void CollectResource(Resource resource)
19     {
20         if (CanCollectResources)
21         {
22             // Check if the resource type already exists in the inventory
23             var existingResource = Inventory
                    .FirstOrDefault(r => r.Type == resource.Type);
24
```
(continued on next page) →

```
25|  → (continued from previous page)
26|
27|        if (existingResource != null)
28|        {
29|            // Update the amount of the existing resource
30|            existingResource.Amount += resource.Amount;
31|        }
32|        else
33|        {
34|            // Add the new resource to the inventory
35|            Inventory.Add(resource);
36|        }
37|
38|        switch (resource.Amount)
39|        {
40|            // Bonus calculation case statements here...
41|        }
42|        Stamina -= staminaNeededToCollect;
43|      }
44|    else  { ... } // Notify user not enough stamina...
45|    }
46|
47|    // Other player methods here...
48| }
```

In line 23, Alex updates the CollectResource method to search the inventory for an existing resource of the same type, using the FirstOrDefault method. FirstOrDefault is part of the LINQ (Language Integrated Query) framework and allows for easier searching through the list. If a matching resource is found, the CollectResource method updates the amount (line 30). If no match is found, the method adds the new resource to the inventory using the Add() method (line 35). Since the list adjusts its size dynamically, there's no need to manage unused slots or worry about running out of space, making the inventory system more efficient.

Testing the Refined Solution

Once Alex has implemented the new List<Resource> system, he tests the solution to ensure that the inventory behaves as expected. He simulates several scenarios collecting multiple resources, as shown in Code Block 7.17.

In this test, Alex confirms that resources are correctly added to the inventory and that the amount of an existing resource is updated when collected again. The lambda expressions passed into the CollectResource method serve as a simple placeholder since the method requires a bonus calculation.

Code Block 7.17: Testing the Revised Inventory System

```
1  Player player = new("Alex");
2
3  // Simulate collecting 10 units of wood
4  Resource wood = new(ResourceType.Wood, 10);
5  player.CollectResource(wood, () => { return 1; });
6
7  // Simulate collecting 5 units of steel
8  Resource steel = new(ResourceType.Steel, 5);
9  player.CollectResource(steel, () => { return 1; });
10
11  // Simulate collecting another 15 units of wood
12  Resource moreWood = new(ResourceType.Wood, 15);
13  player.CollectResource(moreWood, () => { return 1; });
14
15  player.DisplayInventory();
```

By refining the inventory system to use a List<Resource>, Alex has made the game's code more flexible, scalable, and easier to maintain. This optimization lays the groundwork for future expansions, such as adding new types of resources or allowing players to carry larger inventories.

Recap: Structuring Data with Purpose

As Alex progressed through this chapter, he applied the problem-solving strategy of Structuring Data with Purpose to create a well-organized, flexible system for managing collections of resources in his game. By transitioning from an array to a list, Alex improved the efficiency and flexibility of his inventory system, allowing the game to grow without the need to manage fixed sizes or empty slots manually. This approach mirrors the careful organization that we observe in God's creation, where every part has its place, purpose, and function.

We also saw how arrays and two-dimensional arrays could represent data in a structured way, allowing Alex to manage resources and even simulate a crafting grid. By structuring his data carefully, Alex was able to create clean, efficient code that accurately represented the game play mechanics he envisioned.

Finally, Alex refined his solution by using the List<T> collection to manage the player's inventory. This shift gave him more control and flexibility over how resources are stored and managed, ensuring that the system could grow without limitation. Let's add Structuring Data with Purpose to your growing problem-solving toolkit in Text Box 7.4.

Text Box 7.4: Problem–Solving Strategies

1. **Follow the Five-Step Problem-Solving Process**
   Understand the problem, plan the solution, implement the solution, test the solution, and finally refine and optimize it. This structured approach will help you systematically tackle any programming challenge you encounter.

2. **Break Down Big Problems into Smaller Parts**
   Whenever you face a large, complicated problem, break it down into smaller, simpler parts. In programming, this often involves using objects and classes to represent different pieces of the problem. By focusing on one piece at a time, you'll find the overall solution much easier to achieve.

3. **Evaluate Multiple Scenarios**
   Plan for different conditions and map out the appropriate actions for each. This includes identifying the extreme values at the edges of the expected inputs and testing how the program behaves under these conditions.

4. **Repeating with Purpose**
   When designing loops, analyze the tasks to be repeated, identifying what stays consistent (commonality) and what changes (variability) in each iteration. Be intentional about how and why you're repeating actions, and ensure that loops serve a clear purpose, stopping when the goal is achieved.

5. **Establishing Boundaries with Purpose**
   Define variable scope, lifetime, and the structure of your data thoughtfully, ensuring that your program has the right balance between protection and flexibility. Establish clear boundaries in your program's design to protect important variables and maintain control in a way that reduces errors and improves efficiency.

6. **The Expert Pattern**
   Assign responsibility for tasks to the classes or methods that have the most knowledge and control over the task. By delegating behavior to the "experts" in your system, you ensure that your code is well-organized, each piece is responsible for its own duties, and the program remains modular and easy to manage. Use the Expert Pattern to decide where each method belongs and ensure that your code is clear, maintainable, and adaptable as the system grows.

7. **Structuring Data with Purpose**
   When dealing with collections of data, ensure that you choose the appropriate data structure for the task. Arrays, two-dimensional arrays, and lists each have their own strengths and weaknesses. Organize your data thoughtfully, so that your code remains clear, scalable, and easy to manage.

Summary

In this chapter, we explored how to manage collections of data in Alex's game by using arrays, two-dimensional arrays, and lists to store and process information efficiently. Drawing on biblical principles of order and structure, we discussed how data organization in programming mirrors the intentional design we see in creation, where each element serves a purpose and contributes to the whole. Just as God's creation is structured and orderly, the way we manage data in our programs must also be thoughtful and purposeful to ensure clarity, efficiency, and scalability.

We began by introducing arrays to represent the player's inventory of resources, providing a straightforward method to store and manage multiple items of the same type. Arrays allow for easy access and iteration, but they have limitations, such as fixed size, which led us to explore other data structures that provide greater flexibility.

The two-dimensional array concept was then introduced through the idea of a crafting grid in Alex's game. This allowed us to explore how data can be organized in multiple dimensions, and how nested loops can be used to process this type of data structure efficiently. By placing resources in specific positions on a grid, Alex was able to implement more complex game mechanics, such as crafting, while maintaining an organized and efficient code base.

As we moved forward, we refined Alex's solution by replacing the fixed-size inventory array with a dynamic list. This switch allowed Alex to handle a growing inventory without the limitations imposed by an array, while also simplifying the management of resources. We discussed the benefits of using generic lists, including the ability to add and remove items dynamically, and how this shift gave Alex more control over his game's resource management system.

Throughout the chapter, we focused on the problem-solving strategy of Structuring Data with Purpose, emphasizing the importance of choosing the right data structure for each task, whether that be an array, a two-dimensional array, or a list. We highlighted how the choice of structure affects the organization, efficiency, and flexibility of Alex's game, ensuring that it remains scalable as new features are added.

By learning to structure data thoughtfully and choosing the appropriate tools to manage it, Alex was able to create a more organized, efficient, and maintainable system for his game. This approach not only helped him solve the immediate challenges of resource management but also laid a strong foundation for future growth and complexity in his game.

Review Questions

1. What is the difference between an array and a generic list in terms of their flexibility in size?
2. How do you declare and initialize a two-dimensional array in C#, and what scenarios would benefit from using one?
3. Explain how a for loop can be used to process data in an array.
4. What is the advantage of using a generic list over an array when adding or removing items dynamically?
5. Describe a situation where using a generic list would be more beneficial than an array in a real-world application.
6. What are the limitations of arrays in managing dynamic collections of data?
7. How does a nested for loop work, and why would you use one to process a two-dimensional array?
8. What is a generic type in C#, and why are generic lists commonly used to manage collections of objects?
9. In what circumstances would you choose to use a two-dimensional array over a list, and why?
10. How does using lists improve the efficiency and flexibility of storing and managing collections of data?

Practice Problems

1. **Array Initialization and Access**. Write a program that declares an array of integers with five elements. Initialize the array with values and then use a loop to display each value on the screen.

2. **Summing Array Elements**. Write a method that accepts an array of integers and returns the sum of its elements. Use a loop to calculate the sum. Test your method by creating an array of integers, calling the method, and displaying the total sum.

3. **Finding the Maximum Value**. Write a program that accepts an array of integers and finds the maximum value in the array. Output the maximum value to the console.

4. **Two-dimensional Array Creation**. Create a 3x3 two-dimensional array of integers and initialize it with values. Then, use nested loops to display the elements of the two-dimensional array in a grid format.

5. **Average of Array Values**. Write a method that accepts an array of floating-point numbers and returns the average value of the array. Test the method with at least two different sets of numbers.

6. **Two-dimensional Array for Seating Arrangement**. Write a program that simulates a seating arrangement in a classroom, using a two-dimensional array of strings, where each string represents a person's name. Add functionality to assign people to seats, remove a person from the chart when given their name, and display the seating chart.

"What you have heard from me in the presence of many witnesses entrust to faithful men, who will be able to teach others also."
2 Timothy 2:2 (ESV)

CHAPTER 8

REUSING CODE WITH INHERITANCE

Introduction

Throughout Scripture, we see a recurring theme of continuity. God established His work in creation and allows it to continue and grow through the faithful stewardship of His people. One generation's obedience and faithfulness lay the foundation for the next generation to build upon, advancing God's kingdom. In the same way, God calls us to faithfully receive the legacy handed down to us, to be stewards not just of material resources but also of the wisdom, values, and responsibilities passed down through generations.

One example of this kind of continuity is the relationship between Abraham, Isaac, and Jacob in Genesis. God made a covenant with Abraham, promising to bless him and his descendants (Genesis 12:1-3). This covenant was passed down from Abraham to Isaac, and then from Isaac to Jacob. Each patriarch inherited the blessings of God's covenant.

In the New Testament, we see the importance of passing down faith and responsibility. The Apostle Paul, in his letters, emphasizes the idea of spiritual inheritance. He instructs Timothy, his spiritual son, to faithfully carry on the work of the gospel. In 2 Timothy 2:2 (ESV), Paul writes,

"What you have heard from me in the presence of many witnesses entrust to faithful men, who will be able to teach others also." Here we see a model of passing on both knowledge and responsibility, ensuring that the work does not end with one person but continues to grow and flourish through others.

This biblical principle of continuity and trust is deeply connected to our understanding of inheritance. In programming, inheritance allows us to build on the work that has already been established, ensuring that what has come before is not wasted but extended and enhanced. Instead of writing new code from scratch, we inherit functionality from base classes, using what is already working as a foundation to build something new.

Inheritance in programming reflects both the blessing and the responsibility of stewardship. God has entrusted us with gifts, talents, and resources, and we are called to use them wisely. In a similar way, inheritance in programming enables us to build on existing, well-crafted code, using it as a foundation to create something purposeful and efficient. By doing so, we make the most of what we have, adding new value while being efficient with our time and efforts.

Inheritance also ties into a key problem-solving strategy known as Don't Repeat Yourself (DRY). The DRY principle encourages us to minimize repetition in our code by centralizing shared functionality into a single, reusable location. Instead of writing the same code over and over, we inherit existing methods and properties from base classes, focusing on extending and enhancing what has already been built. When we refactor our code to adhere to the DRY principle, we ensure that our programs are more maintainable, readable, and scalable. If a bug is found or an enhancement is needed, we can make the change in one place rather than hunting through the entire code base for duplicated code. This reduces errors and improves efficiency.

By keeping our code DRY, we are being faithful stewards of the work already done, avoiding redundancy and waste. In this chapter, Alex will apply inheritance and the DRY problem-solving strategy to extend the game with new features, refactor his existing structures to be more efficient, and avoid duplicating code.

Step 1. Understand the Problem

As Alex continues to expand his game, he realizes that the game world has grown beyond just collecting resources. While collecting resources like wood, stone, and steel has been a core part of the game, players now need more functionality to progress. Specifically, Alex wants to add new types of objects called Equipment. Equipment includes items such as swords, shields, armor, and tools that players can equip and use to enhance their game play experience. Unlike resources, which are mostly consumed or collected in bulk, equipment has a different role: it can be worn, wielded, or used by the player to gain various benefits, like increasing damage in combat or offering protection from enemies.

The challenge for Alex is that, while equipment and resources are fundamentally different, they also share several overlapping attributes and behaviors. For example, both equipment and resources have names and amounts that provide context to the player. They are both items the player interacts with in the game world. Yet, they differ in their specific uses. A resource like wood can be gathered and crafted into something new, while equipment like a sword can be equipped by the player and used in combat.

Alex recognizes that writing separate code for both resources and equipment would lead to duplication of effort. Much of the logic for storing, naming, and assigning value to resources would need to be copied for equipment as well. However, if Alex were to simply copy and paste the code, it would create a maintenance burden: any future updates or fixes to this common functionality would need to be done in multiple places.

Moreover, the differences between resources and equipment can't be ignored. Equipment will have additional properties that resources don't, such as durability (how long a piece of equipment lasts before breaking) or attack power (how much damage a sword deals in combat). These properties are specific to equipment and don't apply to resources like wood or stone.

Faced with this problem, Alex needs to find a way to reuse the shared functionality between resources and equipment while still accounting for their differences. To do this, Alex must centralize the common attributes (such as names and values) and behaviors (such as interacting with the player) into a shared structure that both resources and equipment can use. At the same time, he needs to ensure that each item type, whether a resource or a piece of equipment, can have its own specific properties and methods.

This leads Alex to the concept of **inheritance**, which will allow him to create a **base class** that contains all the common functionality for both resources and equipment. He can then create specialized classes for each that inherit from the base class and extend the functionality where necessary. This approach will help him keep his code DRY by consolidating shared logic in one place, while also giving him the flexibility to customize the behavior of each type of item.

Step 2. Plan the Solution

As Alex begins to think through the solution, his primary focus is on how to add Equipment to the game while avoiding duplication of code, as discussed earlier. To solve this, Alex decides to create a base class that will contain all the shared attributes and behaviors of both resources and equipment. This base class will act as a foundation that both Resource and Equipment classes can build upon. By using a base class, Alex ensures that all the shared functionality is written only once, making the code more maintainable and easier to expand in the future.

Identifying the "Is-A" Relationship

In object-oriented programming, the relationship between Resource, Equipment, and the new base class is what we call an "Is-A" relationship. This means that both Resource and Equipment can be thought of as specific types of a more general Item class. In this case, Alex will name the base (also called parent) class Item, because both resources and equipment are items that exist in the game. In other words, we can say:

- Resource "Is-A" Item
- Equipment "Is-A" Item

By establishing these "Is-A" relationships, Alex can ensure that the Item class holds all the shared behaviors and properties, such as the name and amount. The Resource and Equipment classes will be derived (also called child) classes, because they inherit the common properties from Item, while adding their own specific attributes and behaviors where necessary.

In a class diagram, an inheritance relationship is depicted using an arrow with an open triangle symbol that starts at the derived class and points to the base class (Item). The Resource and Equipment classes will both point to Item, indicating that they inherit from it.

Distinguishing the "Has–A" Relationship

While an "Is-A" relationship defines inheritance, there's another important relationship Alex will need to consider: the "Has-A" relationship. This relationship describes how one object contains another. For example, in Alex's game, the Player has a collection of Item objects in their inventory. This is a "Has-A" relationship because the player possesses or contains items.

The distinction between these two relationships is important. The "Is-A" relationship is about inheritance and describes the generalization of a class (e.g., a resource or equipment is a specific kind of item). The "Has-A" relationship is about composition, where one class includes instances of another class as part of its definition (e.g., a player has items in their inventory).

In the class diagram, the "Has-A" relationship is represented with a line connecting the two classes, with no arrowhead. For example, there would be a line connecting the Player class to the Item class, indicating that the player *has* an inventory of items.

Figure 8.1: Updated Partial Class Diagram

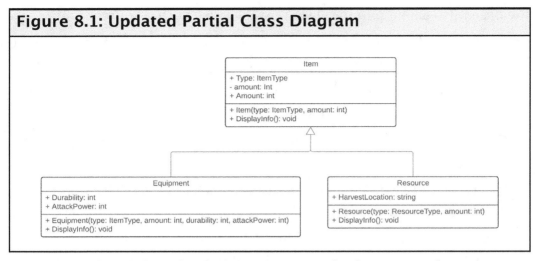

In Alex's updated class diagram in Figure 8.1, he focuses on the inheritance relationships among the Item, Resource, and Equipment classes. The Item class includes all the common properties shared by resources and equipment. The Resource class inherits these shared properties from Item while also adding its own unique attribute and method. Similarly, the new Equipment class inherits from Item and adds attributes that are specific to equipment. The class diagram represents these relationships using an arrow with an open triangle on the end pointing to Item from both Resource and Equipment.

Refactoring for DRY

As Alex starts planning the solution, he can already see the benefits of the DRY (Don't Repeat Yourself) principle. By introducing the Item class, Alex avoids writing the same code multiple times. Instead, he centralizes all the shared functionality for resources and equipment into the Item class, ensuring that any changes to common behavior only need to be made in one place. This approach not only makes the code more efficient but also makes it easier to maintain and extend as Alex continues to add new features to the game.

With this plan in place, Alex is ready to move on to implementing the solution, where he will create the Item class and refactor the existing Resource class to inherit from it. He will then introduce the Equipment class, adding properties like durability and attack power to differentiate it from resources while still leveraging the shared functionality of the `Item` class.

Step 3. Implement the Solution

Now that Alex has outlined the problem and identified the need for a shared `Item` class, he is ready to implement the solution.

The `ItemType` Enumeration

Initially, Alex used an enumeration called `ResourceType` to define various types of resources, such as wood or steel. However, with the addition of equipment items to the game, Alex realizes that both resources and equipment need to be categorized in a similar manner. To address this, he renames `ResourceType` to `ItemType` to better encompass both resources and equipment. This change, shown in Code Block 8.1 allows Alex to standardize item categorization across the game and prevents redundancy.

Code Block 8.1: The `ItemType` Enumeration

```
1  public enum ItemType
2  {
3     None = 0, Stone = 1, Steel = 2, Graphite = 3, Gold = 4, Gemstone = 5,
4     Wood = 6, Copper = 7, Iron = 8, Sand = 9, Sword = 10, Bucket = 11
5  }
```

The Item Class

The `Item` class, shown in Code Block 8.2 holds common properties such as `Amount` and `ItemType`. The `Amount` property tracks the quantity currently held in the player's inventory, while the `Type` attribute categorizes the item into types like wood, steel, armor, or sword. By defining these attributes at the top level, Alex avoids duplicating code and ensures a consistent structure for both resources and equipment. This approach also makes future expansion simpler, as any new item type can inherit these core attributes without needing additional adjustments. Additionally, it keeps the code organized, making it easier to maintain.

Code Block 8.2: The Item Class

```
1  public class Item
2  {
3     // Common properties for all items
4     public ItemType Type { get; set; }
5     private int amount;
6     public int Amount
7     {
8        get
9        {
10          return amount;
11       }
12       set
13       {
14          amount = value >= 0 ? value : 0;
15       }
16    }
17
18    // Constructor for Item class
19    public Item(ItemType type, int amount)
20    {
21       Type = type;
22       Amount = amount;
23    }
24
25    // Method to display item information
26    public virtual void DisplayInfo()
27    {
28       Console.WriteLine($"Type: {Type}");
29       Console.WriteLine($"Amount: {Amount}");
30    }
31 }
```

To initialize these properties, Alex creates a constructor for the Item class that takes parameters for amount and type (lines 19 through 23) This ensures that every item has a defined type and quantity when it is created, providing consistency across all items in the game. He also includes a **virtual** method called DisplayInfo() which prints details like the amount and type of the item (lines 26 through 30). Marking DisplayInfo() as virtual allows subclasses to provide their own version of this method when they override it, enabling each item type to display additional information specific to that item while still ensuring that the common information is displayed consistently across all items.

Refactoring Resource to Inherit from Item

After defining the Item class, Alex turns his attention to refactoring the existing Resource class, shown in Code Block 8.3. By inheriting from the Item class, Resource automatically gains access to the shared properties of `Type` and `Amount`. However, Alex realizes that resources could use an additional property to represent what makes them unique within the game. Each resource could use a `HarvestLocation` attribute to describe where it is typically gathered. For example, wood is harvested from a forest, while iron is collected from a mine. This additional context enriches the player's understanding of the game world, giving a sense of where different materials originate. Alex also ensures the `DisplayInfo()` method for `Resource` includes `HarvestLocation` when displaying the resource's details.

Code Block 8.3: Refactored Resource Class

```
1  public class Resource : Item
2  {
3      public string HarvestLocation { get; set; }
4
5      // Constructor for Resource, which calls the base constructor
6      public Resource(ItemType type, int amount) : base(type, amount)
7      {
8          switch (type)
9          {
10             case ItemType.Wood:
11                 HarvestLocation = "Forest";
12                 break;
13             case ItemType.Stone:
14                 HarvestLocation = "Ground";
15                 break;
16             case ItemType.Steel:
17             case ItemType.Graphite:
18             case ItemType.Gold:
19             case ItemType.Gemstone:
20                 HarvestLocation = "Mine";
21                 break;
22             default:
23                 HarvestLocation = "Unknown";
24                 break;
25         }
26     }
27
28     // Method to display resource-specific information
29     public override void DisplayInfo()
30     {
31         base.DisplayInfo();
32         Console.WriteLine($"Harvest Location: {HarvestLocation}");
33     }
34 }
```

In this version of the `Resource` class, Alex uses inheritance in line 1 by adding : `Item` after the class declaration. This tells C# that `Resource` is a subclass of `Item` and will inherit all of its properties and methods. When Alex designs the `Resource` class to inherit from the `Item` class, he needs to make sure each `Resource` instance is properly set up during construction. Since `Resource` is a type of `Item`, the constructor must first initialize the common properties from `Item` (i.e., `Amount` and `Type`) before adding any specific details, such as `HarvestLocation`. The `base` keyword allows the `Resource` constructor to call the `Item` constructor, ensuring that everything is set up in the correct order, starting with the shared properties and then moving on to the `Resource`-specific attributes. This process of a constructor in the derived (child) class calling the constructor in the base (parent) class, is known as **constructor chaining**.

Constructor chaining is important because it makes sure that all parts of an object are set up in the right order. When a `Resource` is created, it inherits properties from `Item`, and the `base` keyword is what links the `Resource` constructor to the `Item` constructor, allowing the setup to happen seamlessly. Without this connection, Alex would have to repeat the setup for shared properties in each subclass, leading to repetitive and harder-to-manage code.

In situations where the base class has a default constructor (i.e., it doesn't require any parameters), the chaining happens automatically, and there's no need to explicitly use `base`. However, if the base class requires specific values to be set up, like `Amount` and `Type`, using `base` is necessary to make sure everything gets properly initialized.

After calling the base class constructor, the remaining code in the `Resource` constructor runs, where Alex uses a `switch` statement to determine the `HarvestLocation` based on the type of resource. This way, each resource type is given an appropriate harvest location, adding meaningful context for the player. Finally, in line 29 Alex uses the `override` keyword to override the behavior of the `DisplayInfo()` method from the default behavior specified by the `Item` class. The method will now include `HarvestLocation` details, ensuring that when information about a resource is displayed, the player gets a complete picture of the resource's origin and quantity.

The Equipment Class

With the `Resource` class updated, Alex then creates the `Equipment` class in Code Block 8.4, which also inherits from `Item`. Unlike `Resource`, which focuses on collection and quantity, equipment has attributes related to its utility in the game. Alex decides that each piece of equipment should have the properties `Durability` and `AttackPower`. Durability indicates how long the item can be used before wearing out, while attack power provides context for swords used in combat. To ensure the information is conveyed clearly to the player, Alex updates the `DisplayInfo()` method for equipment, adding the specific details about `Durability` and `AttackPower` to the output, building on the base `DisplayInfo()` method from the `Item` class.

Code Block 8.4: The Equipment Class

```
 1  public class Equipment : Item
 2  {
 3      // Additional properties unique to Equipment
 4      public int Durability { get; set; }
 5      public int AttackPower { get; set; }
 6
 7      // Constructor for Equipment, which calls the base constructor
 8      public Equipment(int amount, ItemType type, int durability,
          int attackPower) : base(type, amount)
 9      {
10          Durability = durability;
11          AttackPower = attackPower;
12      }
13
14      // Method to display equipment-specific information
15      public override void DisplayInfo()
16      {
17          base.DisplayInfo();
18          Console.WriteLine($"Durability: {Durability}");
19          Console.WriteLine($"Attack Power: {AttackPower}");
20      }
21  }
```

Updating to an Inventory of Items

Once Alex has the updated `Item`, `Resource`, and `Equipment` classes, he integrates them into the player's inventory system, as shown in Code Block 8.5. Previously, the inventory was limited to storing only resources, but now that both `Resource` and `Equipment` are derived from `Item`, Alex takes advantage of polymorphism to create a more versatile inventory.

Code Block 8.5: Updated Player Class

```
1   public class Player
2   {
3      private List<Item> inventory;
4
5      // Other Player Properties and Fields...
6
7      public bool AddToInventory(Item item)
8      {
9         var existingItem = inventory.FirstOrDefault(i => i.Type == item.Type);
10        if (existingItem != null)
11        {
12           existingItem.Amount += item.Amount;
13           Console.WriteLine($"{item.Amount} {item.Type} added to inventory.");
14           Console.WriteLine($"Total: {existingItem.Amount}");
15        }
16        else
17        {
18           inventory.Add(item);
19           Console.WriteLine($"{item.Type} has been added to your inventory.");
20        }
21        return true;
22     }
23
24     public bool HasInInventory(ItemType itemType)
25     {
26        return inventory.Any(item => item.Type == itemType);
27     }
28
29     public void DisplayInventory()
30     {
31        Console.WriteLine("Inventory:");
32
33        // Loop through each item in the inventory array
34        for (int index = 0; index < inventory.Count; index++)
35        {
36           if (inventory[index] != null)
37           {
38              // Display details of the item if it's not null
39              Console.WriteLine($"Slot {index + 1}:");
40              inventory[index].DisplayInfo();
41           }
42        }
43     }
44
45     // Other Player methods here...
46  }
```

Polymorphism allows different types derived from a common base class to be treated as if they were instances of their base class, while retaining their own identity. In this case, both Resource and Equipment can be treated as Item objects, meaning Alex can use a single inventory list to store both types seamlessly. He updates the Player class to store items as a list of Item objects in line 3, allowing the player to carry a mix of resources and equipment. This new approach is more efficient and reduces code duplication.

The `AddToInventory()` method in lines 7 through 22 in the `Player` class is designed to add both resources and equipment. By using the `FirstOrDefault()` method, it checks if an item of the same `ItemType` already exists in inventory (line 9). If a match is found, the method updates the existing item by increasing its amount and notifying the player with the new total (lines 12 through 14). Otherwise, the new item is added as a separate entry in the inventory (lines 18 and 19). This logic ensures that similar items are stacked together, while new items are efficiently added. This streamlined approach allows Alex to manage all inventory items through a single, unified system.

The `HasInInventory()` method provides an efficient way to check if a particular type of item exists in the player's inventory. By using the `Any()` method that is part of the LINQ framework, Alex can determine if the inventory contains an item of the specified type without needing to manually iterate through each slot. This method further simplifies item management, making it easy to verify whether a player has certain resources available for crafting or other game play actions.

By integrating these changes, Alex creates an inventory system that is flexible enough to accommodate both resources and equipment while maintaining clear, organized code that minimizes redundancy. The new design allows the player's inventory to grow with the game, adapting to the challenges and opportunities that come with crafting, collecting, and equipping items.

Updating the Crafting System

With the new inheritance structure in place, Alex also revisits the `CraftingSystem` class to incorporate the `Item` class and ensure that crafted items can be added to the player's inventory. The first change Alex makes is to update the `Result` property in the `Recipe` class to be an `Item` object, reflecting the possibility of crafting both resources and equipment, as shown in Code Block 8.6.

Code Block 8.6: Updated Recipe Class

```
1  public class Recipe
2  {
3    public string Name { get; set; }
4    private ItemType[,] pattern;
5    public Item Result { get; private set; }
6
7    public Recipe(string name, ItemType[,] pattern, Item result)
8    {
9      Name = name;
10     this.pattern = pattern;
11     Result = result;
12   }
13
14   // Method to check if the current grid matches the recipe pattern
15   public bool Matches(ResourceType[,] grid)
16   {
17     for (int row = 0; row < 3; row++)
18     {
19       for (int column = 0; column < 3; column++)
20       {
21         if (grid[row, column] != Pattern[row, column])
22         {
23           return false;  // If any cell doesn't match, the recipe fails
24         }
25       }
26     }
27     return true;  // If all cells match, the recipe is valid
28   }
29 }
```

Next, Alex updates the `Craft` method in the `CraftingSystem` class to return the crafted `Item`, instead of a `Resource`, as shown in Code Block 8.7.

Code Block 8.7: Updated CraftingSystem Class

```
1  // Method to attempt crafting
2  public Item Craft()
3  {
4    foreach (var recipe in recipes)
5    {
6      if (recipe != null && recipe.Matches(craftingGrid))
7      {
8        Console.WriteLine($"Crafted {recipe.Name}!");
9        return recipe.Result;
10     }
11   }
12   Console.WriteLine("No matching recipe found.");
13   return null;
14 }
```

Step 4. Test the Solution

Now that Alex has implemented the inheritance structure, it's time for him to test his solution to ensure that everything works as expected.

Alex's goal is to verify that the Player class can now handle both resources and equipment in the player's inventory.

The first test Alex runs is to create instances of both Resource and Equipment and add them to the player's inventory. Since both classes inherit from Item, the player's inventory should be able to store a mix of resources and equipment, taking advantage of polymorphism.

Alex begins by creating a new Player object. He then creates two Resource objects (wood and stone) and adds them to the player's inventory using the CollectResource method. Code Block 8.8 shows the code Alex uses to test adding resources.

Code Block 8.8: CollectResource Tests

```
1  Player player = new Player("Alex");
2
3  Resource wood = new Resource(ItemType.Wood, 10);
4  Resource moreWood = new Resource(ItemType.Wood, 15);
5  Resource stone = new Resource(ItemType.Stone, 5);
6
7  player.CollectResource(wood, () => { return 1; });
8  player.CollectResource(moreWood, () => { return 1; });
9  player.CollectResource(stone, () => { return 1; });
```

When Alex runs the program, he checks the output to confirm that both resources are successfully added to the player's inventory. The expected result is that CollectResource calls AddToInventory, which prints messages indicating that each resource has been added, as shown in Text Box 8.1.

Text Box 8.1: CollectResources Test Output

Wood has been added to your inventory.
15 Wood added to inventory.
Stone has been added to your inventory.

Next, Alex wants to test whether the Equipment class works correctly in the player's inventory (see Code Block 8.9). In line 2, he creates an instance of Equipment, which is a sword with a durability of 50 and an attack power of 25, and adds it to the player's inventory in line 3. Since Equipment also inherits from Item, the inventory can store it without any issues.

Code Block 8.9: AddToInventory Test

```
1| Player player = new Player("Alex");
2| Equipment sword = new Equipment(1, ItemType.Sword, 50, 25);
3| player.AddToInventory(sword);
```

Again, Alex checks the output to confirm that the sword has been successfully added to the inventory, as shown in Text Box 8.2.

Text Box 8.2: AddToInventory Test Output

Sword has been added to your inventory.

The next step in testing is to ensure that the Player class can display all the items in the inventory, whether they are resources or equipment. Alex uses the DisplayInventory() method to print the details of each item starting by printing the inventory slot number. The DisplayInventory() method then calls the DisplayInfo() method of each item. Since both Resource and Equipment inherit from Item, they share the DisplayInfo method, but each also overrides it to include unique details. The Resource class adds the HarvestLocation, and Equipment includes the durability and attack power. Alex uses the code in Code Block 8.10 to add a piece of equipment and a resource before displaying the player's inventory.

Code Block 8.10: DisplayInventory Test

```
1| Player player = new Player("Alex");
2|
3| Equipment sword = new Equipment(1, ItemType.Sword, 50, 25);
4| player.AddToInventory(sword);
5|
6| Resource wood = new Resource(ItemType.Wood, 10);
7| player.CollectResource(wood, () => { return 1; });
8|
9| player.DisplayInventory();
```

The expected output should show the details of both items. For the wood (Resource object), the output displays its type, amount, and harvest location. For the sword (Equipment object), the output includes additional details like durability and attack power, as shown in Text Box 8.3.

With these tests, Alex confirms that the inheritance structure works as intended. The Player class now properly handles both resources and equipment, leveraging the shared `Item` base class. The `CollectResource` and `AddToInventory` methods behave as expected, and the program successfully displays item details in the inventory using polymorphism. This ensures that Alex's game has the flexibility needed to manage different types of items efficiently, without duplicating code.

Text Box 8.3: `DisplayInventory` Test Output

Sword has been added to your inventory.
Wood has been added to your inventory.
Keep going to reach your goal.
Inventory:
Slot 1:
Type: Sword
Amount: 1
Durability: 50
Attack Power: 25
Slot 2:
Type: Wood
Amount: 10
Harvest Location: Forest

Step 5. Refine and Optimize

As Alex refines his game, he explores further improvements he can make, focusing on using the inheritance structure more effectively. The new `Item` base class allows for additional optimizations that enhance the game play experience and make the code more manageable.

Code Block 8.11: `IsInventoryFull` Method

```
private int maxInventorySize = 10;

public bool IsInventoryFull
{
    get
    {
        return inventory.Count >= maxInventorySize;
    }
}
```

One of the first refinements Alex considers is re-introducing an upper limit for the player's inventory capacity. One of the side-effects of using an array earlier was that arrays required us to specify a maximum size. Alex preferred that strategy, but that was lost when he made the transition to using a list. To reinstate this functionality, Alex adds a new IsInventoryFull computed property to the Player class, as shown in Code Block 8.11.

Alex adjusts the AddToInventory() method to check if the inventory is at its capacity before attempting to add more items. Additionally, since the player's inventory no longer contains a resources with an item type of None, Alex decides to add a check to ensure these are not mistakenly added to the player's inventory. This ensures that the inventory stores only valid and meaningful items, preventing unintended bugs.

Code Block 8.12: Updated AddToInventory Method

```
 1  public bool AddToInventory(Item item)
 2  {
 3    if (item.Type == ItemType.None)
 4    {
 5      Console.WriteLine("Invalid item: None cannot be added to inventory.");
 6      return false;
 7    }
 8
 9    if (IsInventoryFull)
10    {
11      Console.WriteLine("Your inventory is full! You cannot add more items.");
12      return false;
13    }
14
15    var existingItem = inventory.FirstOrDefault(i => i.Type == item.Type);
16    if (existingItem != null)
17    {
18      existingItem.Amount += item.Amount;
19      Console.WriteLine($"{item.Amount} {item.Type} added to inventory.");
20      Console.WriteLine($"Total: {existingItem.Amount}");
21    }
22    else
23    {
24      inventory.Add(item);
25      Console.WriteLine($"{item.Type} has been added to your inventory.");
26    }
27    return true;
28  }
```

Recap: Don't Repeat Yourself (DRY)

In this chapter, Alex applied the problem-solving strategy known as Don't Repeat Yourself (DRY) to streamline and optimize his code. The DRY principle emphasizes the importance of reducing redundancy and avoiding unnecessary repetition in our code by centralizing shared functionality into reusable components. By applying inheritance to his game's structure, Alex ensured that both the Resource and Equipment classes could share common properties and behaviors, inheriting them from a base class. This allowed him to build upon existing structures without having to duplicate code in each class.

Moreover, when refactoring the player's inventory system, Alex further implemented the DRY principle by leveraging the power of lists and LINQ to simplify common operations such as checking inventory space, adding items, and crafting resources. By eliminating repetitive loops and replacing them with concise and expressive code, Alex made the game's functionality more efficient and maintainable.

The DRY principle is foundational to writing clean, scalable, and maintainable code. It encourages us to consolidate logic that will be used in multiple places, ensuring that changes can be made in one location rather than across multiple, duplicated code segments. DRY isn't just about code efficiency—it's also about promoting good stewardship of the code we write, ensuring that it can grow and evolve without unnecessary complications or redundancy. Let's add Don't Repeat Yourself (DRY) to your growing problem-solving toolkit in Text Box 8.4.

Summary

In this chapter, we explored the powerful concept of inheritance in programming, a tool that allows us to build upon existing code structures while maintaining efficiency and clarity. Inheritance allows classes to share common properties and methods from a base class, enabling us to avoid redundant code and implement new features more efficiently. This aligns with the principle of stewardship, where we make the most of the resources entrusted to us.

We began by examining a conceptual problem in Alex's game: the need to introduce new items, such as equipment, that share some attributes with resources but also possess distinct behaviors. By using

Text Box 8.4: Problem–Solving Strategies

1. **Follow the Five-Step Problem-Solving Process**
   Understand the problem, plan the solution, implement the solution, test the solution, and finally refine and optimize it.

2. **Break Down Big Problems into Smaller Parts**
   Whenever you face a large, complicated problem, break it down into smaller, simpler parts. In programming, this often involves using objects and classes to represent different pieces of the problem.

3. **Evaluate Multiple Scenarios**
   Plan for different conditions and map out the appropriate actions for each. This includes identifying the extreme values at the edges of the expected inputs and testing how the program behaves under these conditions.

4. **Repeating with Purpose**
   When designing loops, analyze the tasks to be repeated, identifying what stays consistent (commonality) and what changes (variability) in each iteration. Be intentional about how and why you're repeating actions, and ensure that loops serve a clear purpose, stopping when the goal is achieved.

5. **Establishing Boundaries with Purpose**
   Define variable scope, lifetime, and the structure of your data thoughtfully, ensuring that your program has the right balance between protection and flexibility. Establish clear boundaries in your program's design to protect important variables and maintain control in a way that reduces errors and improves efficiency.

6. **The Expert Pattern**
   Assign responsibility for tasks to the classes or methods that have the most knowledge and control over the task. Use the Expert Pattern to decide where each method belongs and ensure that your code is clear, maintainable, and adaptable as the system grows.

7. **Structuring Data with Purpose**
   When dealing with collections of data, ensure that you choose the appropriate data structure for the task. Arrays, two-dimensional arrays, and lists each have their own strengths and weaknesses. Organize your data thoughtfully, so that your code remains clear, scalable, and easy to manage.

8. **Don't Repeat Yourself (DRY)**
   Centralize shared functionality into reusable components to avoid code duplication. This strategy ensures that you can make changes in one place and have them reflected across the entire program, leading to more efficient, maintainable, and scalable code.

inheritance, Alex was able to define a common base class, Item, from which both Resource and Equipment inherited shared properties like name, type, and value, while also gaining the flexibility to add new properties or behaviors specific to each subclass. This solved the problem of needing to manage similar data and behavior across different item types without duplicating code.

Through inheritance, we saw how Alex could build a hierarchy of classes that enabled the game to grow in complexity while keeping the code base clean and efficient. This is where the Don't Repeat Yourself (DRY) principle became crucial. By centralizing shared logic in the `Item` base class, Alex could focus on the unique behaviors for each derived class, such as defining how equipment could be equipped by the player or used in crafting, without needing to repeat shared functionality.

Additionally, we explored how lists and LINQ can be combined with inheritance to manage player inventories more effectively. By using LINQ to search, filter, and manipulate the inventory of items, Alex's game became not only more efficient but also easier to extend and maintain.

In summary, this chapter demonstrated the importance of inheritance as a tool for code reuse and organization, helping us manage complex data relationships without duplicating work. It also underscored the significance of the DRY principle in creating maintainable, scalable systems that can grow with the needs of the program.

Review Questions

1. What is the primary purpose of using inheritance in object-oriented programming?
2. How does inheritance help us apply the Don't Repeat Yourself (DRY) principle in programming?
3. Explain the difference between a base class and a derived class and provide an example different from the one discussed in the chapter.
4. In the context of Alex's game, what shared attributes did the Resource and Equipment classes inherit from the Item base class?
5. What is the difference between an "Is-A" relationship and a "Has-A" relationship in object-oriented programming?

6. What are the risks of overusing inheritance, and how can we avoid them while still benefiting from code reuse?

7. How does the proper use of inheritance in programming reflect the biblical principle of stewardship?

Practice Problems

1. **Basic Inheritance Setup**. Create a base class called Vehicle with common attributes such as make, model, and year. Then, create two derived classes: Car and Motorcycle. The Car class should have an additional property for numberOfDoors, while the Motorcycle class should have an additional property for hasSidecar. Implement constructors for all classes and write a program to create instances of each and display their properties.

2. **Overriding Methods**. Build on Problem 1. Add a method to the Vehicle base class called StartEngine that prints a message like "The engine is starting." Override the StartEngine method in both the Car and Motorcycle classes to display a different message for each type of vehicle.

3. **Polymorphism**. Create a Tool base class with an abstract method Use(). Then create two derived classes: Hammer and Screwdriver. Implement the Use() method in each derived class, printing a message that describes how the tool is being used. Write a program that stores both Hammer and Screwdriver objects in a list and uses polymorphism to call their respective Use() methods in a loop.

4. **Base Class for a Game**. For a simple game, create an Entity base class that has properties for Name and Health. Then, create two derived classes: Player and Enemy. The Player class should have additional properties such as Stamina, while the Enemy class should have an additional property for AttackPower. Write methods in the Entity class to display the current status of an entity, and test it by creating both Player and Enemy objects.

5. **Refactor Code Using Inheritance**. Refactor the following scenario using inheritance: You have two separate classes, Cat and Dog, each with the properties Name and Age, and a MakeSound() method. They both make different sounds, but share the same attributes. Create a Pet base class to avoid repetition, and implement MakeSound() for both Cat and Dog, so that the method prints the kind of sound that the animal makes on the console.

6. **Constructor Chaining**. Create a Person base class with properties for FirstName and LastName. Add a constructor that accepts both properties. Then, create a Student derived class that also has a GPA property. Use constructor chaining to initialize both the Person and Student class properties, and write a program to create and display student details.

7. **Adding Methods to the Base Class**. Create a class hierarchy with a base class Shape and two derived classes: Rectangle and Circle. Add a CalculateArea() method to the base class that is overridden by each derived class to calculate the area of the specific shape. Write a program that stores both Rectangle and Circle objects in a list and uses polymorphism to call their respective CalculateArea() methods in a loop.

"And let us not grow weary of doing good, for in due season we will reap, if we do not give up."
Galatians 6:9 (ESV)

Appendices

Exploring Advanced Concepts

Congratulations on completing the first eight chapters of this book! At this stage, you should have a strong grasp of problem-solving using programming concepts, as well as a solid understanding of how these principles were applied to Alex's game.

The following appendices are designed for readers who want to explore some of the more advanced topics in programming. Each appendix builds on what you've already learned, offering deeper insights and new tools to expand your coding capabilities. These sections do not follow the same structured five-step problem-solving approach from the main chapters but rather focus on specific techniques that can enhance Alex's game and provide you with practical experience tackling more complex challenges.

Each appendix begins with the assumption that you've completed the first eight chapters and are ready to go further. The appendices are short, targeted, and practical, introducing key concepts, demonstrating their relevance with simple examples, and integrating them into Alex's game to enrich its functionality. Let's continue the journey!

APPENDIX A

RECURSION

Introduction

In this appendix, we explore the concept of recursion and its practical application in Alex's game. Recursion is a technique where a method calls itself to solve a problem by breaking it down into smaller, more manageable parts. It's particularly useful when problems involve repeated tasks or hierarchical dependencies. This approach helps simplify complex problems by allowing us to focus on solving smaller instances of the same task, building up to the overall solution step by step.

To illustrate recursion, consider a classic mathematics problem: calculating the factorial of a number. The factorial of a number n (denoted as $n!$) is the product of all positive integers from one to n. For example, 5! equals $5 \times 4 \times 3 \times 2 \times 1$, which equals in 120. A recursive approach is ideal for calculating factorials because each factorial value can be expressed as a smaller instance of itself: $n! = n \times (n - 1)!$. This is where the concept of recursion shines. Solving for $n!$ requires the same process as solving a smaller problem, $(n - 1)!$.

Understanding the Call Stack

Before we get into the practical applications of recursion, it is important to understand the concept of the call stack. The **call stack** works like a stack of plates in a cafeteria, where each plate represents a method call. When a new method is called, it is added to the top of the stack, and when the method completes, it is removed from the stack. This mechanism follows a Last In, First Out (LIFO) principle. The call stack plays an essential role in keeping track of the sequence of method calls and their execution order.

To illustrate the call stack, Code Block A.1 shows a program with three methods: FirstMethod, SecondMethod, and ThirdMethod. The program starts by executing FirstMethod, which then calls SecondMethod, and subsequently, SecondMethod calls ThirdMethod.

Code Block A.1: Call Stack Example

```
 1| public class CallStackExample
 2| {
 3|    // Main entry to the program
 4|    public static void Main(string[] args)
 5|    {
 6|       FirstMethod();
 7|    }
 8|
 9|    public static void FirstMethod()
10|    {
11|       Console.WriteLine("In FirstMethod");
12|       SecondMethod();
13|       Console.WriteLine("Exiting FirstMethod");
14|    }
15|
16|    public static void SecondMethod()
17|    {
18|       Console.WriteLine("In SecondMethod");
19|       ThirdMethod();
20|       Console.WriteLine("Exiting SecondMethod");
21|    }
22|
23|    public static void ThirdMethod()
24|    {
25|       Console.WriteLine("In ThirdMethod");
26|    }
27| }
```

Figure A.1 illustrates the change in the call stack in this example. The program begins with the Main method as the first method on the call stack (a). When FirstMethod is called, it is added to the stack (b). Next,

Figure A.1: Call Stack

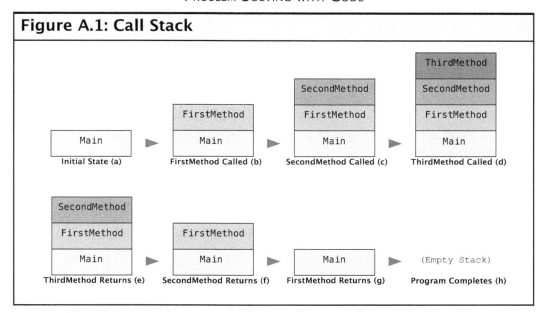

SecondMethod is called from within FirstMethod, so it is added to the top of the stack, while Main and FirstMethod remains underneath (c). When SecondMethod calls ThirdMethod, it is added to the top of the stack as well (d). Now, the stack contains three methods: FirstMethod, SecondMethod, and ThirdMethod, with ThirdMethod at the top.

As ThirdMethod completes its execution, it is removed from the stack (e), and control returns to SecondMethod, which continues executing until it also finishes and is removed (f). Finally, the program returns to FirstMethod, and once it completes, the only item left on the stack is the program's entry point (g). Once the Main method finishes, the call stack is empty, indicating that the program has finished running (h). The call stack ensures that each method is executed in the correct order, managing each call until it is complete.

Recursion and the Call Stack

The concept of the call stack is particularly important in recursion. In a recursive function, the same method repeatedly calls itself, and each call is added to the stack. To understand how this works, let's start by looking at an example of improper recursion and why it can lead to a problem called a stack overflow. Consider the silly example in Code Block A.2.

Code Block A.2: Example of Improper Recursion

```
1  public void SillyMethod()
2  {
3     Console.WriteLine("Calling myself...");
4     SillyMethod(); // The method calls itself with no condition to stop.
5  }
```

In this example, SillyMethod calls itself without any condition to terminate the calls. When this method is executed, it continues calling itself over and over again, each time adding a new instance of SillyMethod to the call stack. Without a proper stopping condition, the stack grows larger and larger. Since the call stack has a finite size, there is only so much space available for adding "plates" (or method calls). Eventually, the stack reaches its maximum capacity and cannot accommodate any more calls. This results in a stack overflow error called a StackOverflowException, a point where the memory allocated for the stack is exceeded.

To make recursion work, it is critical to identify and implement a base case. The **base case** is a condition that stops the recursion. This base case ensures that the recursion eventually stops, allowing the call stack to start unwinding. Without this base case, as we saw in SillyMethod, the stack would continue to grow uncontrollably, eventually leading to a failure.

With that understanding, let's return to the example of calculating a factorial that we introduced at the beginning of this appendix. In the case of factorial, the base case is the simplest of all factorials, when $n = 1$, because $1! = 1$. Thus, the recursion ends at one and returns this value without further calling itself.

Code Block A.3 shows how we can write a recursive method to calculate the factorial of a number in C#. The Factorial method calls itself with the parameter n - 1 until it reaches n == 1. The base case ensures that the recursion stops at one, while the recursive case multiplies the current value n by the result of Factorial(n - 1). If we call Factorial(5), it evaluates like this: $5 * 4 * 3 * 2 * 1$, resulting in 120.

Code Block A.3: Recursive Factorial Method

```
 1  public int Factorial(int n)
 2  {
 3     // Base case: if n is 1, return 1
 4     if (n == 1)
 5     {
 6        return 1;
 7     }
 8     // Recursive case: n * (n - 1)!
 9     return n * Factorial(n - 1);
10  }
```

Another example that demonstrates recursion is the Fibonacci sequence. In the Fibonacci sequence, each number is the sum of the two preceding ones. It starts with 0, 1, 1, 2, 3, 5, 8, 13, and so on. Mathematically, the nth Fibonacci number is defined by two base cases: Fibonacci(0) = 0 and Fibonacci(1) = 1. For any n > 1, the value of Fibonacci(n) is given by Fibonacci(n - 1) + Fibonacci(n - 2). This repeated, layered dependency makes recursion a natural choice for calculating Fibonacci numbers. In the code, the base cases stop the recursion by returning values for Fibonacci(0) and Fibonacci(1). The recursive case computes Fibonacci(n) by summing the results of two smaller problems, Fibonacci(n - 1) and Fibonacci(n - 2). Code Block A.4 shows a simple implementation of a recursive Fibonacci method.

Code Block A.4: Recursive Fibonacci Method

```
 1  public int Fibonacci(int n)
 2  {
 3     // Base cases
 4     if (n == 0)
 5     {
 6        return 0;
 7     }
 8     if (n == 1)
 9     {
10        return 1;
11     }
12     // Recursive case: F(n) = F(n - 1) + F(n - 2)
13     return Fibonacci(n - 1) + Fibonacci(n - 2);
14  }
```

While this implementation of the Fibonacci sequence is elegant, it is also inefficient due to the multiple redundant calls for the same values. Each call to Fibonacci results in exponential growth in the number of recursive calls, which can slow down performance significantly. This example serves as a reminder that although recursion is a powerful technique, it may not always be the optimal solution when problems involve overlapping sub-problems. In such cases, iterative methods may be more suitable for efficiency.

Recursion Applied

To integrate recursion into Alex's game, he starts by focusing on the crafting system, which presents an ideal scenario for recursive programming due to its layered dependencies. In many crafting systems, complex items require several intermediate components, creating multiple layers of requirements. For example, to craft a shield, a player may first need to create steel plates, which in turn require steel as a raw material. Alex's goal is to implement an automatic crafting feature for these complex recipes, where the system breaks down the crafting process into smaller steps for the player. Recursion offers an elegant solution to manage these dependencies seamlessly.

Alex begins by updating the Recipe class by adding a new method called GetRequiredItems. This new method traverses the pattern array and generates a list of items needed for crafting. This method consolidates the quantities of each item, avoiding redundancy by adding amounts together when the same item type appears multiple times in the pattern. This approach allows Alex to easily determine the resources required without manually counting each item. Code Block A.5 shows the revised Recipe class.

Code Block A.5: The Revised Recipe Class

```
 1| public class Recipe
 2| {
 3|    public string Name { get; set; }
 4|    private ItemType[,] pattern;
 5|    public Item Result { get; private set; }
 6|
 7|    public Recipe(string name, ItemType[,] pattern, Resource result)
 8|    {
 9|      Name = name;
10|      this.pattern = pattern;
11|      Result = result;
12|    }                                    (continued on next page) →
```

```
13|  → (continued from previous page)
14|
15|    public List<Item> GetRequiredItems()
16|    {
17|      List<Item> requiredItems = new();
18|      for (int row = 0; row < 3; row++)
19|      {
20|        for (int column = 0; column < 3; column++)
21|        {
22|          ItemType currentType = pattern[row, column];
23|          if (currentType != ItemType.None)
24|          {
25|            var existingItem = requiredItems
      ↳        .FirstOrDefault(item => item.Type == currentType);
26|            if (existingItem != null)
27|            {
28|              existingItem.Amount++;
29|            }
30|            else
31|            {
32|              requiredItems.Add(new Item(currentType, 1));
33|            }
34|          }
35|        }
36|      }
37|      return requiredItems;
38|    }
39| }
```

Next, Alex turns his attention to the CraftingSystem class, which will orchestrate the recursive crafting logic. The crafting system needs to determine whether the player can craft a requested item, and if not, recursively craft the intermediate components until the final item can be made. To achieve this, Alex implements a method called CraftItem that accepts the player instance and the name of the item to be crafted, as shown in Code Block A.6.

Code Block A.6: Updated CraftingSystem Class

```
1|  public class CraftingSystem
2|  {
3|    private List<Recipe> recipes = new();
4|    private ItemType[,] craftingGrid = new ItemType[3, 3]; // 3x3 crafting grid
5|
6|    public CraftingSystem()
7|    {
8|      ClearGrid();  // Initialize the crafting grid to be empty (None)
9|      // Define example recipes
10|     recipes.Add(new Recipe("Steel Plate", new ItemType[,]
11|     {
12|       { ItemType.Steel, ItemType.Steel, ItemType.Steel },
13|       { ItemType.Steel, ItemType.Steel, ItemType.Steel },
14|       { ItemType.Steel, ItemType.Steel, ItemType.Steel }
15|     }, new Resource(ItemType.SteelPlate, 1)));
16|
```
(continued on next page) →

```
17|  → (continued from previous page)
18|
19|      recipes.Add(new Recipe("Solid Wood", new ItemType[,]
20|      {
21|        { ItemType.Wood, ItemType.Wood, ItemType.Wood },
22|        { ItemType.Wood, ItemType.Wood, ItemType.Wood },
23|        { ItemType.Wood, ItemType.Wood, ItemType.Wood }
24|      }, new Resource(ItemType.SolidWood, 1)));
25|
26|      recipes.Add(new Recipe("Shield", new ItemType[,]
27|      {
28|        { ItemType.SolidWood, ItemType.SteelPlate, ItemType.SolidWood },
29|        { ItemType.SteelPlate, ItemType.SteelPlate, ItemType.SteelPlate },
30|        { ItemType.SolidWood, ItemType.SteelPlate, ItemType.SolidWood }
31|      }, new Equipment(ItemType.Shield, 1, 200, 5)));
32|    }
33|
34|    public bool CraftItem(Player player, ItemType itemType)
35|    {
36|      Recipe recipe = recipes.FirstOrDefault(r => r.Result.Type == itemType);
37|      if (recipe == null)
38|      {
39|        Console.WriteLine($"Recipe for {itemType} not found.");
40|        return false;
41|      }
42|
43|      List<Item> requiredItems = recipe.GetRequiredItems();
44|
45|      // Base case: If player has all items needed, craft the item
46|      if (requiredItems.All(req => player.HasInInventory(req)))
47|      {
48|        foreach (Item req in requiredItems)
49|        {
50|          player.RemoveFromInventory(req);
51|        }
52|        player.AddToInventory(recipe.Result);
53|        Console.WriteLine($"Successfully crafted: {itemType}");
54|        return true;
55|      }
56|
57|      // Recursive case: Craft the components first
58|      foreach (Item req in requiredItems)
59|      {
60|        while (!player.HasInInventory(req))
61|        {
62|          Console.WriteLine($"Need to craft {req.Type} for {itemType}");
63|          if (!CraftItem(player, req.Type))
64|          {
65|            Console.WriteLine($"Cannot craft {req.Type}. Missing resources.");
66|            return false;
67|          }
68|        }
69|      }
70|
71|      // After crafting necessary components, craft the main item
72|      return CraftItem(player, itemType);
73|    }
74|
75|    // Other Crafting System Methods Here...
76|  }
```

After retrieving the requested recipe, the `CraftItem` method checks if the player has all the items required to craft the requested item (line 46), which represents the base case of the recursion. If the player has all the items, the required quantities are removed from the inventory, and the crafted item is added to the player's inventory. If the player does not have all the required items, the method enters a recursive process to craft the needed components (line 58). The `foreach` loop iterates over each required item, and the nested while loop ensures that the missing components are crafted until the player has enough of each required item. Once all the components have been crafted, the method calls itself again to craft the main item because it couldn't be crafted earlier due to missing components (line 72). This final call ensures that, once all parts are available, the crafting process is completed successfully.

Let's walk through an example of how this code would execute when crafting a shield, assuming the player starts with only 100 units of steel and 50 units of wood in their inventory. When the player attempts to craft a shield, the `CraftItem` method is called with the `ItemType.Shield`. The method first checks if there is a recipe for a shield (line 36), which it finds. Then, the method calls `GetRequiredItems` on the shield recipe (line 43), which returns a list of items: four solid wood and five steel plates.

Since the player does not have any solid wood or steel plates, the recursive case is triggered. The foreach loop starts with the first required item (line 58), which is a steel plate, and the while loop continues until enough steel plates are available (line 60). The crafting system will recursively call `CraftItem` again (line 63), this time with `ItemType.SteelPlate`, adding the new call to the call stack. Since the player has sufficient steel, the crafting system creates the steel plates by removing the appropriate amount of steel from the inventory (line 50), adds the steel plate to the inventory (line 52), and returns `true` to the first `CraftItem` method call on the call stack, where it continues the while loop until enough steel plates have been crafted.

Once all the steel plates are crafted, the while loop condition is met, so the `foreach` loop moves to the next required item, which is solid wood.

The crafting system recursively calls `CraftItem` again (line 63), this time with `ItemType.SolidWood`, adding it to the call stack. Since the player has enough wood in their inventory, the crafting system creates the solid wood by removing the required wood from the inventory and adding the solid wood to the inventory, and then returning once again to the first `CraftItem` call. Once all the required items have been crafted, the `foreach` loop in line 58 finishes, and the crafting system makes a final recursive call to `CraftItem` to craft the shield itself, using the newly crafted components. The crafted shield is then added to the player's inventory, completing the process.

This implementation makes the crafting experience easier for the player and keeps the code more maintainable by using recursion to handle dependencies. The recursive logic ensures that all necessary components are crafted before the final item. With this approach, Alex has made the crafting system more efficient, user-friendly, and capable of handling complex recipes while keeping resource gathering an important part of the game.

Testing the Recursion

To validate the functionality of the newly implemented crafting system, Alex knows that he should test his solution. This test will verify that the `CraftItem` method successfully handles both simple and complex crafting scenarios, including recursive crafting of intermediate components. As shown in Code Block A.7, the testing process begins with the creation of a new player instance named "Alex." Initially, the player's inventory is empty, so Alex needs to add resources to prepare for crafting. He adds 100 units of steel and 50 units of wood, which should be enough to craft a shield. With the initial setup complete, Alex creates an instance of the `CraftingSystem` (line 9), and he uses the system to craft a shield (line 13), since he knows that a shield requires some intermediate components that must be crafted first.

Code Block A.7: Testing the CraftItem Method

```
1 | // Create a player instance
2 | Player player = new Player("Alex");
3 |
4 | // Add some initial resources to the player's inventory
5 | player.AddToInventory(new Resource(ItemType.Steel, 100));
6 | player.AddToInventory(new Resource(ItemType.Wood, 50));
7 |
8 | // Create a crafting system instance
9 | CraftingSystem craftingSystem = new CraftingSystem();
10 |
11 | // Test crafting an even more complex item (Shield)
12 | Console.WriteLine("\n--- Attempting to Craft Shield ---");
13 | craftingSystem.CraftItem(player, ItemType.Shield);
```

Upon running the test, the CraftItem method is executed, triggering the crafting sequence. Since the shield requires solid wood and steel plates, neither of which are directly available in Alex's inventory, the crafting system will need to create these components before crafting the final shield. The crafting system uses the steel and wood in Alex's inventory to craft the required steel plates and solid wood through a series of recursive calls. Once all the necessary components are crafted, the system makes a final call to craft the shield and adds it to the player's inventory.

The console output, shown in Text Box A.1 provides feedback at each stage, including messages indicating the crafting of intermediate components, followed by a successful crafting message for the shield itself. The results of the test confirm that the crafting system works well for complex, multi-layered items, confirming that the recursive logic efficiently handles all necessary crafting steps. This testing not only validates the correctness of the code but also demonstrates the enhanced crafting experience for the player, eliminating the need for tedious manual steps.

Summary

In this appendix, we explored how recursion can be effectively integrated into Alex's game to streamline the crafting system. Recursion is a powerful tool that allows a function to solve a problem by breaking it into

Text Box A.1: CraftItem Test Output

--- Attempting to Craft Shield ---
Need to craft SolidWood for Shield
9 Wood removed from your inventory.
SolidWood has been added to your inventory.
Successfully crafted: SolidWood
Need to craft SolidWood for Shield
9 Wood removed from your inventory.
1 SolidWood added to inventory.
Total: 2
Successfully crafted: SolidWood
Need to craft SolidWood for Shield
9 Wood removed from your inventory.
1 SolidWood added to inventory.
Total: 3
Successfully crafted: SolidWood
Need to craft SolidWood for Shield
9 Wood removed from your inventory.
1 SolidWood added to inventory.
Total: 4
Successfully crafted: SolidWood
Need to craft SteelPlate for Shield
9 Steel removed from your inventory.
SteelPlate has been added to your inventory.
Successfully crafted: SteelPlate
Need to craft SteelPlate for Shield
9 Steel removed from your inventory.
1 SteelPlate added to inventory.
Total: 2
Successfully crafted: SteelPlate
Need to craft SteelPlate for Shield
9 Steel removed from your inventory.
1 SteelPlate added to inventory.
Total: 3
Successfully crafted: SteelPlate
Need to craft SteelPlate for Shield
9 Steel removed from your inventory.
1 SteelPlate added to inventory.
Total: 4
Successfully crafted: SteelPlate
Need to craft SteelPlate for Shield
9 Steel removed from your inventory.
1 SteelPlate added to inventory.
Total: 5
Successfully crafted: SteelPlate
4 SolidWood removed from your inventory.
5 SteelPlate removed from your inventory.
Shield has been added to your inventory.
Successfully crafted: Shield

smaller, similar sub-problems. By employing recursion, Alex was able to develop an automatic crafting system that manages dependencies for complex items without needing extensive, procedural code for each individual crafting step.

The core of this implementation lies in the recursive `CraftItem` method, which breaks down a crafting request into smaller tasks, crafting intermediate components as needed. We walked through an example where Alex attempted to craft a shield, which required multiple recursive calls to craft solid wood and steel plates. By recursively calling the `CraftItem` method, Alex's game ensures that all components are prepared before the final item is crafted.

Testing confirms that the recursive crafting logic works as intended, allowing the player to automatically craft layered items like the shield, while still maintaining the need for the player to collect base-level resources such as steel and wood. Overall, the use of recursion in the crafting system not only simplifies the crafting experience but also results in a more efficient and maintainable code base.

APPENDIX B

Nullable Types

Introduction

In this appendix, we explore the concept of nullable types and their practical application in Alex's game. Nullable types provide a way to handle situations where a value might be absent or undefined, which is common in many real-world programming scenarios. In C#, value types such as integers and booleans cannot usually represent a "null" value. However, by using nullable types, we can give these value types the flexibility to represent an absence of data. This is especially useful when dealing with optional fields or when a value is not always applicable.

To illustrate nullable types, let's consider a simple example of tracking a person's age. Normally, age is represented by an integer, but what if we don't know someone's age yet? Instead of setting it to an arbitrary number like zero (which could be misleading), we can use a nullable integer to indicate that the age is currently unknown. In C#, this can be done with the `int?` syntax, which allows us to represent either a numeric age value or `null`. This approach makes the code more expressive and reduces potential misunderstandings or errors due to ambiguous placeholder values.

In Alex's game, nullable types can be used to handle cases where certain items or values are conditionally available. For example, when tracking which resource is currently selected by the player, it may be possible that no resource is selected at a given time. Using a nullable type allows us to represent this "no selection" state clearly, without relying on arbitrary placeholder values. This approach not only makes the code more readable but also reduces the likelihood of errors due to unexpected default values. Before we explore how Alex can use nullable types to enhance his game's logic, let's first examine how nullable types can be used in C# along with their related operators.

Using Nullable Types in Code

Let's first explore how to declare, assign, and work with nullable types in C#. We'll then cover some helpful operators and techniques to manage nullable values effectively.

Declaring Nullable Types

To create a nullable type, we use the ? symbol after the value type. For example, if we want an integer that can also represent a missing value, we declare it as shown in Code Block B.1.

Code Block B.1: Declaring a Nullable Type

```
1| int? optionalNumber = null;
```

In this example, optionalNumber can hold either an integer value or null, indicating the absence of a value. This is different from a standard int, which must always have a value.

Key Properties and Operations

When we declare a variable as a nullable type, C# behind the scenes wraps the variable inside a Nullable<T> generic structure. This structure provides two key properties to manage its values: HasValue and Value. The HasValue property indicates whether the nullable type currently holds a value. As shown in Code Block B.2, if HasValue is true, we can use the `Value` property to retrieve the actual value. Accessing `Value` when `HasValue` is `false`, however, will result in an error that will cause your program to crash.

Code Block B.2: Accessing Nullable Properties

```
int? score = 85;
if (score.HasValue)
{
    Console.WriteLine("Score: " + score.Value);
}
else
{
    Console.WriteLine("Score is not available.");
}
```

Null–Coalescing Operator (??)

The null-coalescing operator (??) allows us to provide a default value in case a nullable type is `null`. This is particularly useful to avoid null checks and provide fallback values more concisely, as shown in Code Block B.3. In line 2, if `optionalScore` is `null`, `finalScore` will be set to 0. The ?? operator makes the code simpler and easier to read.

Code Block B.3: Using the Null–Coalescing Operator

```
int? optionalScore = null;
int finalScore = optionalScore ?? 0;
Console.WriteLine("Final Score: " + finalScore);
```

Null–Conditional Operator (?.) and Null Chaining

Another useful operator when working with nullable types is the **null-conditional operator** or **null-chaining operator** (?.). This operator allows us to access members of an object only if it is not `null`. It is particularly handy when working with chains of properties or method calls that may contain null values at any point, as shown in Code Block B.4.

Code Block B.4: Null–Conditional Operator

```
Player? player = null;
string? playerName = player?.Name;
```

In this example, line 1 creates a nullable `Player` object and assigns it the value of `null`. In line 2, the null chaining operator is used to test if the player object is `null`. If `player` is `null` at this point, the null chaining operator will cause the entire right hand side of the statement to equal `null` and assign that `null` value to `playerName`. This is a convenient way to safely navigate objects that may not be initialized.

Nullable Types Applied

Nullable Types can bring considerable benefits to Alex's game, particularly in areas where the absence of a value needs to be represented more explicitly. One excellent application is in the crafting grid, which uses an enum value `ItemType.None` to indicate an empty slot. By using nullable types, Alex can streamline the code and remove the need for this placeholder value, making the system more intuitive and reducing potential confusion.

Using a specific enum value like `None` to represent an empty slot leads to more complex logic, requiring constant checks to see if a particular cell is holding `None` or a legitimate resource, as well as checks to exclude `None` from being collected as a resource or added to the player's inventory. This extra logic not only added clutter to the code but also made it more error-prone.

By making each slot in the crafting grid a nullable type, such as `ItemType?`, Alex can simplify the code considerably. Instead of having to check if the value in a slot is `ItemType.None`, the code can directly check if the slot is `null` and make use of the null coelescing and null chaining operators. This approach also provides a more natural way to represent an empty slot, since an absence of a value is more accurately indicated by `null`. Code Block B.5 shows an example of how the crafting grid can be defined using a nullable `ItemType`.

Code Block B.5: Updated Crafting Grid Definition

```
1│ ItemType?[,] craftingGrid = new ItemType?[3, 3];
```

With this new approach, checking whether a slot is empty becomes more straightforward, as shown in Code Block B.6. This not only reduces complexity but also makes the code more readable and maintainable. By removing the need for an artificial None value, Alex's code can now work more naturally with actual game elements, and the crafting logic can focus on handling real resources rather than checking for special cases.

Code Block B.6: Checking if a Grid Slot is Empty

```
1 | // Checking if a given slot is empty
2 | if (craftingGrid[row, column] == null)
3 | {
4 |   Console.WriteLine("This slot is empty.");
5 | }
```

Nullable types also open up opportunities to use the null-coalescing (??) and null-conditional (?.) operators effectively, further simplifying the code. For instance, Alex could use the null-coalescing operator to provide a default value when attempting to read from the crafting grid, as shown in Code Block B.7.

Code Block B.7: Using the Null–Coelescing Operator

```
1 | ItemType selectedItem = craftingGrid[row, column] ?? ItemType.Wood;
2 | Console.WriteLine($"Selected item: {selectedItem}");
```

In this example, if the slot at [row, column] is null, the selected item defaults to ItemType.Wood. This helps avoid null reference issues and provides a fallback behavior when needed.

The null-conditional operator can also be applied to safely navigate and manipulate the crafting grid, as shown in Code Block B.8. Here, if the value in the specified slot is not null, the ToString() method is called. Otherwise, the code safely does nothing, avoiding potential runtime exceptions. This makes handling nullable values concise and helps Alex focus on implementing game logic without constantly worrying about null checks.

Code Block B.8: Using the Null–Conditional Operator

```
1 | craftingGrid[row, column]?.ToString();
```

Summary

In this appendix, we explored the concept of nullable types and how they can enhance both the functionality and readability of Alex's game. By using nullable types, Alex was able to eliminate the need for placeholder enum values, like `ItemType.None`, and instead represent empty slots in the crafting grid more intuitively using `null`. This change not only made the code cleaner and more efficient but also reduced the likelihood of bugs stemming from special-case logic.

We also discussed practical applications of the null-coalescing and null-conditional operators, which provide simplified ways to handle potentially null values. These tools help make the code more expressive and robust, reducing the complexity of managing empty or missing values in the game.

Overall, introducing nullable types into the crafting system has allowed Alex to create a more natural and straightforward representation of empty slots, simplifying both the crafting logic and the player's experience. This adjustment exemplifies how a small change in data representation can significantly impact the clarity and maintainability of the code.

APPENDIX C

USING DICTIONARIES

Introduction

In this appendix, we will explore the use of dictionaries and how they can be applied effectively in Alex's game. Dictionaries are a powerful data structure in programming, allowing us to store and quickly look up key-value pairs. This makes them incredibly useful when managing collections of data that need to be accessed based on unique identifiers rather than by a simple index, like in arrays or lists.

To illustrate the basic idea behind dictionaries, consider a simple example: a collection of student grades. In an array or list, you could store the grades, but it would be difficult to directly look up a specific student's grade without going through the entire collection, one grade at a time. With a **dictionary**, however, you can use the student name or ID as the key and the student's grade as the value. This makes finding a specific student's grade fast and easy, without needing to loop through everything.

Dictionaries are ideal for situations where we need to perform rapid lookups or store values that are uniquely associated with a particular identifier. A dictionary can also make code easier to understand by removing the need for looping and conditionals to find specific items in a collection.

Before we see how Alex can use dictionaries in his game to help manage the game's crafting recipes, the next section will introduce how to use dictionaries in code.

Using Dictionaries in Code

Dictionaries in C# store and manage data in pairs, where each pair consists of a key and a corresponding value. You can think of a dictionary like a contact list on your phone, where you use a person's name (the key) to look up their phone number (the value). This kind of key-value pairing makes dictionaries especially useful when you want to quickly retrieve information without searching through a long list.

To create a dictionary in C#, you need to specify both the key type and the value type. For example, you could create a dictionary to store student grades using the code shown in Code Block C.1.

Code Block C.1: Creating a Dictionary

```
1  using System.Collections.Generic;
2  Dictionary<string, int> grades = new();
```

In this example, the keys are string (student's names), and the values are int (their grades). Using a dictionary like this allows you to quickly find out someone's age by simply looking them up by name. However, creating a new dictionary only creates the structure where the data will be stored; it doesn't add any data to the dictionary. To add values to a dictionary, you use the Add() method, as shown in Code Block C.2.

Code Block C.2: Adding Values to a Dictionary

```
1  grades.Add("Alice", 95);
2  grades.Add("Bob", 69);
3  grades.Add("Charlie", 83);
```

Now, the dictionary contains three key-value pairs: "Alice" is linked to 95, "Bob" is linked to 69, and "Charlie" is linked to 83. If you want to find out Alice's grade, you can use her name as the key, as shown in Code Block C.3.

Code Block C.3: Accessing Values in a Dictionary

```
1 int aliceGrade = grades["Alice"];
2 Console.WriteLine($"Alice's Grade: {aliceGrade}");
```

If you try to access a key that isn't in the dictionary, it will cause an error and your program will crash. To avoid this, it's a good idea to check if the key exists before accessing it, using the ContainsKey() method, as shown in Code Block C.4. In this code, line 1 checks to see if there is an entry in the dictionary for George. In this case, George was never added, so this will evaluate to false, and so the else condition (lines 6 through 9) will display a message that George is not in the dictionary.

Code Block C.4: Verifying Existence of Keys in a Dictionary

```
1 if (grades.ContainsKey("George"))
2 {
3    int georgeGrade = grades["George"];
4    Console.WriteLine($"George's Grade: {georgeGrade}");
5 }
6 else
7 {
8    Console.WriteLine("George is not in the dictionary.");
9 }
```

Another common operation is updating values. Suppose Bob's instructor wanted to award Bob 10 points of extra credit. You can update his score, as shown in Code Block C.5. In this code, the expression on the right first retrieves the current value in the grades dictionary for Bob, then it adds 10 to that value, and finally, it assigns the new score to Bob's entry in the dictionary.

Code Block C.5: Updating Values in a Dictionary

```
1 grades["Bob"] = grades["Bob"] + 10;
```

You can also remove entries from a dictionary. If you want to remove Bob from the dictionary, you use the Remove() method, as shown in Code Block C.6.

Code Block C.6: Removing Entries from a Dictionary

```
1| grades.Remove("Bob");
```

A great feature of dictionaries is the ability to loop through all elements of the dictionary individually. Each dictionary entry is represented by an instance of the KeyValuePair object. The KeyValuePair object provides two properties: Key, which represents the key of the entry, and Value, which represents the value stored in that entry. This makes it easy to access both parts of each entry while iterating through the dictionary. For example, if you want to print out everyone's name and grade, you can use a foreach loop to iterate through each key value pair, as shown in Code Block C.7. This makes it easy to see all the data stored in your dictionary.

Code Block C.7: Iterate through All Dictionary Entries

```
1| foreach (var kvp in ages)
2| {
3|     Console.WriteLine($"Name: {kvp.Key}, Age: {kvp.Value}");
4| }
```

Dictionaries Applied

Let's explore how Alex can use in his game. Dictionaries help organize data efficiently, especially in areas where quick lookups are needed. One particular place where Alex can make good use of dictionaries is in storing and managing the player's inventory.

Currently, Alex's inventory is represented as a list, where each item is stored individually. When the player collects a resource or adds an item, the code has to loop through the list to check if the item already exists. If it does, the code then updates the quantity of that item. This approach can lead to clunky code, especially as the game grows more complex and more items are added. Each time an item is added or removed, the list has to be searched, which can become inefficient and cumbersome to manage.

By converting the inventory into a dictionary, Alex can use the `ItemType` as a key and store the quantity as the value. This way, instead of iterating through the entire list to find a specific item, the game can directly access the item using its key. This not only makes the code cleaner but also significantly improves performance, particularly as the number of items grows. The updated inventory might look like the code shown in Code Block C.8.

Code Block C.8: Updated Inventory in Player Class

```
1 | private Dictionary<ItemType, int> inventory = new();
```

Using a dictionary for inventory management means that adding or updating items becomes much simpler. For example, if the player collects 10 units of wood, the code can easily check if wood is already in the inventory and update the quantity accordingly, as shown in Code Block C.9.

Code Block C.9: Updating Inventory Items

```
1 | if (inventory.ContainsKey(ItemType.Wood))
2 | {
3 |    inventory[ItemType.Wood] += 10;
4 | }
5 | else
6 | {
7 |    inventory.Add(ItemType.Wood, 10);
8 | }
```

This approach ensures that items are always stored in a consistent way, without the risk of duplicating entries or needing to manage empty slots. To see how this change simplifies the `Player` class, let's revisit some of the existing methods. For example, the `AddToInventory` method becomes more streamlined, as shown in Code Block C.10.

Code Block C.10: Updated AddToInventory Method

```
1 | public bool AddToInventory(Item item)
2 | {
3 |    if (item.Type == ItemType.None)
4 |    {
5 |       Console.WriteLine("Invalid item: None cannot be added to inventory.");
6 |       return false;
7 |    }
8 |
```
(continued on next page) →

```
 9|  → (continued from previous page)
10|
11|    if (inventory.ContainsKey(item.Type))
12|    {
13|        inventory[item.Type] += item.Amount;
14|        Console.WriteLine($"{item.Amount} {item.Type} added to inventory. Total:
   ↵       {inventory[item.Type]}");
15|    }
16|    else
17|    {
18|        inventory.Add(item.Type, item.Amount);
19|        Console.WriteLine($"{item.Type} has been added to your inventory with
   ↵       amount: {item.Amount}");
20|    }
21|    return true;
22| }
```

Similarly, the RemoveFromInventory method can also benefit from using a dictionary. Removing items becomes straightforward since the dictionary allows direct access to each item's quantity, as shown in Code Block C.11.

Code Block C.11: Updated RemoveFromInventory Method

```
 1| public bool RemoveFromInventory(Item item)
 2| {
 3|    if (inventory.ContainsKey(item.Type))
 4|    {
 5|        if (inventory[item.Type] >= item.Amount)
 6|        {
 7|            inventory[item.Type] -= item.Amount;
 8|            if (inventory[item.Type] == 0)
 9|            {
10|                inventory.Remove(item.Type);
11|            }
12|            Console.WriteLine($"{item.Amount} {item.Type} removed from your
   ↵           inventory.");
13|            return true;
14|        }
15|        else
16|        {
17|            Console.WriteLine($"Not enough {item.Type} to remove.");
18|            return false;
19|        }
20|    }
21|    else
22|    {
23|        Console.WriteLine($"{item.Type} not found in inventory.");
24|        return false;
25|    }
26| }
```

By using dictionaries, Alex can eliminate the need for looping through lists to find items, making the code more efficient and less error-prone. The inventory management becomes cleaner, as each item is uniquely identified by its key. This reduces the complexity of the code and makes it easier to maintain.

Summary

In this appendix, we explored the concept of dictionaries and how they can be effectively used in Alex's game. We began by introducing dictionaries as a powerful way to store key-value pairs, allowing for efficient lookups and management of data. Through practical examples, we showed how dictionaries can simplify and optimize code by reducing the need for iterative searches and handling complex data structures more effectively.

We then applied these concepts to Alex's game by converting the player's inventory from a list to a dictionary. This change provided significant improvements in both code maintainability and performance. By using ItemType as the dictionary key, we ensured that items could be added, updated, and removed with ease, eliminating the need for cumbersome iteration and reducing redundancy in the inventory management logic.

APPENDIX D

PROGRAMMING INTERFACES

Introduction

In this appendix, we will explore programming interfaces, a powerful concept in object-oriented programming that can greatly improve the flexibility and scalability of your code. Note that when we refer to "interfaces" in this context, we are not talking about user interfaces (UIs) but rather a specific construct in programming that defines a contract for how certain classes should behave. This distinction is important to avoid confusion, as interfaces play a very different role compared to graphical interfaces that users interact with.

Interfaces are a way to define the capabilities of a class without dictating how those capabilities must be implemented. Imagine an interface as a blueprint for certain behaviors that multiple classes can adopt. By defining a set of methods that a class must implement, an interface ensures that different classes can share a common behavior, allowing you to write more modular, reusable, and testable code. For example, an interface in a sports application might define actions like Score() or Pass(). Any sport that implements this interface would need to provide specific ways to perform these actions. This means that whether you are dealing with basketball, soccer, or hockey, the Score() method can be invoked on any sport that implements the interface, but the way they score is different for each sport. Similarly, in programming, different classes implement the same methods in ways that suit their unique characteristics.

To understand how interfaces can be helpful, consider a scenario where you need different types of items in your game to all be usable in different ways. By creating an interface, you allow these varied items to share a consistent set of behaviors without making them part of the same inheritance hierarchy, which might not make logical sense for their distinct roles. This is one of the key advantages of interfaces: they allow you to group related behaviors in a flexible way, without being bound by rigid inheritance.

In the next section, we will look at some simple examples of interfaces to illustrate their importance and understand how they can be utilized effectively in programming. Then, in the section after that, we will discuss how Alex can use interfaces to enhance his game, specifically focusing on how they can make interacting with game objects more efficient and consistent. By the end of this appendix, you'll have a solid grasp of how interfaces can improve your programs, make them more adaptable, and ensure that your code is organized in a clear and extensible manner.

Using Interfaces in Code

Interfaces can seem abstract at first, so we'll use a simple example to help clarify their value. To begin, let's define a basic interface. An **interface** specifies a set of methods that a class must implement if it chooses to adhere to that interface. Imagine we need different objects to perform a Move() action, like vehicles, animals, or robots. We could define an interface called IMovable to represent the concept of something that can move, as shown in Code Block D.1.

Here, IMovable is the interface, and it defines one method: Move(). The code on line 3 contains the method signature for the Move() method.

The signature includes the method return type, method name, and the list of parameters the method requires. Any class that wants to implement IMovable must define the implementation for the Move() method and its signature must match the one defined in the interface. This interface doesn't dictate how the Move() action is carried out (notice that there are no curly braces to identify the method's behavior). The interface only defines the requirement that a class must have a Move() method with a void return type and no parameters.

Code Block D.1: The IMovable Interface

```
1  public interface IMovable
2  {
3    void Move();
4  }
```

The naming convention for interfaces in C# is to start with a capital "I." This convention helps immediately identify the type as an interface when reading the code, making it clear that IMovable is a contract rather than a concrete implementation. This consistency improves readability and makes it easier for developers to understand the structure of the program, especially in large projects where interfaces play a critical role in defining behaviors.

Next, let's create two different classes, a Car and a Bird, both of which implement the IMovable interface, as shown in Code Block D.2.

Code Block D.2: Implementing an Interface

```
1  public class Car : IMovable
2  {
3    public void Move()
4    {
5      Console.WriteLine("The car drives forward.");
6    }
7  }
8
9  public class Bird : IMovable
10  {
11    public void Move()
12    {
13      Console.WriteLine("The bird flies through the sky.");
14    }
15  }
```

Both Car and Bird implement the IMovable interface by including the : IMovable text after the class name (lines 1 and 9). However, each provides its own version of the Move() method. When we call Move() on a Car object, it prints "The car drives forward." When we call Move() on a Bird object, it prints "The bird flies through the sky." This demonstrates how different classes can share the same behavior but have their own unique implementation. By using an interface, we ensure that any object that implements IMovable will have a Move() method, allowing us to work with these objects in a consistent way.

To see the true power of interfaces, consider a method that can handle any IMovable object. We can write a method called MakeItMove() that accepts an IMovable parameter, as shown in Code Block D.3.

Code Block D.3: Using Interfaces as Method Parameters

```
1|  public void MakeItMove(IMovable movable)
2|  {
3|     movable.Move();
4|  }
```

Now, we can call MakeItMove() with either a Car or a Bird, and it will execute the appropriate Move() method, as shown in Code Block D.4.

Code Block D.4: Passing Objects as Interfaces

```
1|  Car myCar = new();
2|  Bird myBird = new();
3|
4|  MakeItMove(myCar);   // Output: The car drives forward.
5|  MakeItMove(myBird);  // Output: The bird flies through the sky.
```

By using the IMovable interface, we don't need to write separate methods for handling cars or birds. Instead, we write one method that works with any object that implements IMovable. The MakeItMove() method doesn't need to know whether it is working with a Car or a Bird; it simply calls the Move() method, and the appropriate implementation runs.

In this way, interfaces provide a way to work with different types of objects in a consistent and generalized manner. They allow us to design systems that are both flexible and easy to extend, ensuring that adding new types of `IMovable` objects in the future, such as a `Robot` or a `Boat`, is straightforward. This kind of modularity is at the core of what makes interfaces such a powerful tool in object-oriented programming.

Interfaces Applied

In Alex's game, there are various items that players collect and manage in their inventory. These items include consumable resources, like food, and equippable items, like shields and swords. Rather than handling each type separately, Alex can use an interface to define a shared set of properties that all inventory items must have, ensuring consistency across all items. Let's introduce an interface called `IInventoryItem`. This interface will define a few properties and methods that any inventory item must have, such as `Name`, `Weight`, and a method to `GetDescription()`. Code Block D.5 shows the definition of the `IInventoryItem` interface. This interface acts as a contract that any inventory item must adhere to, ensuring consistency across all items in the game.

Code Block D.5: The `IInventoryItem` Interface

```
1  public interface IInventoryItem
2  {
3      string Name { get; }
4      double Weight { get; }
5      string GetDescription();
6  }
```

Next, let's implement this interface for a couple different item types: `Sword` and `Apple`. As shown in Code Block D.6, each of these classes implement the `IInventoryItem` interface with their own implementations.

Code Block D.6: Implementing the `IInventoryItem` Interface

```
1   public class Sword : IInventoryItem
2   {
3       public string Name { get; } = "Sword";
4       public double Weight { get; } = 10.0;
5
6       public string GetDescription()
7       {
8           return "A sharp blade, useful for close combat.";
9       }
10  }
```
(continued on next page) →

```
29|  → (continued from previous page)
30|
31|  public class Apple : IInventoryItem
32|  {
33|     public string Name { get; } = "Apple";
34|     public double Weight { get; } = 0.2;
35|
36|     public string GetDescription()
37|     {
38|        return "A fresh apple that restores energy when eaten.";
39|     }
40|  }
```

In this example, Sword and Apple both implement the IInventoryItem interface. The Sword class provides its own values for Name and Weight, and returns a description indicating its use in combat. Similarly, the Apple class provides its own values, describing how it restores energy when eaten. By using this interface, Alex can manage different types of inventory items more easily in the Player class. Code Block D.7 shows how Alex might revise the inventory property in the Player class to use a list of IInventoryItem.

With this implementation, Alex has transformed the inventory list to hold any items that implement the IInventoryItem interface. This means that the Player class can now handle items like Sword, Apple, and Shield uniformly, making it much easier to add new items to the game in the future.

Using an interface makes Alex's code more organized and extensible. Instead of writing separate methods to handle each type of inventory item, Alex can now use the shared interface to add, remove, and interact with items consistently. This reduces redundancy and makes it easier to add new items to the game without modifying the existing code. It also ensures that all items share the common behaviors defined by the interface, enhancing maintainability in Alex's growing code base.

Interfaces vs. Inheritance

In Chapter 8, we used inheritance by creating a base class called Item, which both Resource and Equipment extended. This approach allowed us to share common properties, such as Name and Amount, across different types of items, helping to avoid code duplication. While inheritance is powerful, it has its limitations, especially when we start thinking about flexibility and reuse.

Code Block D.7: Revised Player Class to use an Interface

```
 1| public class Player
 2| {
 3|   private List<IInventoryItem> inventory;
 4|
 5|   public Player(string playerName)
 6|   {
 7|     inventory = new List<IInventoryItem>();
 8|     Name = playerName;
 9|     // Other initialization logic...
10|   }
11|
12|   // Adding an item to the inventory
13|   public bool AddToInventory(IInventoryItem item)
14|   {
15|     if (inventory.Count >= maxInventorySize)
16|     {
17|       Console.WriteLine("Your inventory is full! Cannot add more items.");
18|       return false;
19|     }
20|
21|     inventory.Add(item);
22|     Console.WriteLine($"{item.Name} has been added to your inventory.");
23|     return true;
24|   }
25|
26|   // Displaying the inventory
27|   public void DisplayInventory()
28|   {
29|     Console.WriteLine("Inventory:");
30|     foreach (var item in inventory)
31|     {
32|       Console.WriteLine($"- {item.Name}: {item.GetDescription()} (Weight:
        {item.Weight})");
33|     }
34|   }
35| }
```

The primary limitation of using a base class is that it enforces a strict hierarchy. Each class can only inherit from one base class, which can become a constraint when we want different items to share specific behavior that doesn't fit neatly into a single inheritance structure. For example, in our game, we might have items that can be both consumable (like food) and equippable (like armor). If we only use inheritance, we'd need a complex class hierarchy that quickly becomes unmanageable, trying to combine different functionalities into the base class.

By introducing interfaces, we gain flexibility that inheritance alone doesn't offer. Interfaces allow a class to implement multiple, shared behaviors without being bound to a single inheritance hierarchy. In other words, an item can implement multiple interfaces, enabling it to take on several roles. For instance, an item could implement IInventoryItem, IUsable, or other interfaces that define particular behaviors, which cannot be done with inheritance alone.

Additionally, using interfaces makes the code easier to extend and maintain. For instance, by defining IInventoryItem, Alex can now add entirely new categories of items, like Clothing or Tools, which implement IInventoryItem without changing the existing inheritance structure. There's no need to make potentially breaking changes to the base class or update classes that don't need new properties or methods. Interfaces enable each class to stay focused on its core purpose while still conforming to shared behaviors.

Another significant advantage is how the interface provides a clear contract. With IInventoryItem, we guarantee that every inventory item has Name and Weight properties and a GetDescription() method. This guarantees consistency across different items, meaning the Player class can handle items uniformly. With inheritance, there's a risk of cluttering the base class with properties or methods that don't necessarily apply to all derived types, but with interfaces, Alex can keep things organized and focused.

Summary

In this appendix, we explored the concept of programming interfaces and how they can bring flexibility and clarity to Alex's game. Interfaces, unlike traditional inheritance, allow us to define shared behaviors across multiple classes without binding them to a rigid hierarchy. By using an interface like IInventoryItem, Alex can introduce new item types and behaviors without disrupting the existing structure, ensuring consistency and improving code reusability. We also looked at how interfaces can help simplify item management, giving Alex the ability to uniformly interact with different types of items while maintaining the unique characteristics of each.

This approach provides a powerful way to keep the code organized, scalable, and easy to extend, allowing the game to grow seamlessly. Using both inheritance and interfaces in tandem ensures that the game code stays efficient and adaptable, providing a solid foundation for future updates and enhancements.

APPENDIX E

FILE INPUT/OUTPUT

Introduction

In this final appendix, we explore the concept of File Input/Output (I/O), which is a powerful tool that allows us to store and retrieve data from files. Many of the programming examples so far have focused on solving problems within the computer's memory. File I/O, however, allows us to work with data that persists beyond the program's execution. This makes it possible for our programs to save information that can be accessed later, even after the program has stopped running.

File I/O also allows us to automate tasks that might otherwise be tedious. Imagine you have a folder full of music files, and you want to create a list of all the songs you have. Instead of typing each song title manually, you could write a program that reads all the file names in the folder and saves them to a text file. This not only saves time but also reduces the chances of making mistakes.

Another useful concept related to File I/O is **JSON** (JavaScript Object Notation), a lightweight data format commonly used for storing and exchanging information. Conceptually, JSON is a structured way to represent data in a readable and organized manner. It is composed of key-value pairs, allowing data to be represented similarly to objects in many programming languages. JSON is often used in file input/output operations because it can easily represent complex structures, such as lists or nested objects, in a format that both humans and computers can understand.

Serialization is the process of converting an object or data structure into a format that can be easily stored or transmitted, such as JSON. For example, a list of contacts could be serialized into JSON so that it can be saved to a file and loaded later, preserving details such as names, phone numbers, and addresses. **Deserialization** is the opposite process, where we convert a JSON representation back into an object that can be used by the program. This is especially useful for storing objects with complex data structures in files because the JSON format keeps the structure intact, making it easy to restore the original object when needed.

Using File Input/Output in Code

In this section, we will explore how to use File Input/Output (I/O) in code by looking at a simple, everyday example. File I/O is a fundamental feature that allows programs to interact with files, either by writing data to a file or reading data from it. The `System.IO` namespace in C# provides the tools necessary for handling files and directories, including reading from and writing to files. Within this namespace, the `File` class provides a number of static methods that make working with files straightforward, allowing us to easily manage data storage and retrieval.

To illustrate these concepts, let's consider a scenario where you want to write a shopping list to a text file. Imagine you are creating a program to help manage your shopping list, and you want to save the items you plan to buy to a file so that you can access them later. In C#, you can do this using the `File.WriteAllText` or `File.AppendAllText` methods. Code Block E.1 shows an example of how you can write this shopping list data to a file. In this example, the `File.WriteAllText` method is used to create a new text file called "shoppingList.txt" and write the contents of the shoppingList variable to it. If the file already exists, WriteAllText will overwrite its content; otherwise, a new file will be created. Once the code runs, the shopping list is saved to the file, and you will see a message confirming that the file was saved.

Code Block E.1: Writing Data to a File

```
1  using System;
2  using System.IO;
3
4  string filePath = "shoppingList.txt";
5  string shoppingList = "- Apples\n- Bread\n- Milk\n- Eggs";
6
7  // Write shopping list to file
8  File.WriteAllText(filePath, shoppingList);
9
10 Console.WriteLine("Shopping list saved to file.");
11
```

Another option for writing data to a file is using File.AppendAllText, which adds new content to an existing file rather than overwriting it. This is useful if you want to add more items to your shopping list without losing any previous data. Code Block E.2 shows an example of how to append an item to the shopping list file. In this snippet, File.AppendAllText is used to add "- Butter" to the end of the shopping list without erasing the existing items. This way, your shopping list keeps growing as you add more items.

Code Block E.2: Appending Data to a File

```
1  using System;
2  using System.IO;
3
4  string filePath = "shoppingList.txt";
5  string newItem = "- Butter\n";
6
7  // Append new item to the shopping list file
8  File.AppendAllText(filePath, newItem);
9
10 Console.WriteLine("New item added to shopping list.");
```

Next, let's discuss how to read data from a file. Suppose you want to read your shopping list back from the file and display it in your program. You can achieve this using the File.ReadAllText method, as shown in Code Block E.3. In this code, the File.ReadAllText method is used to read all the contents of "shoppingList.txt" and store them in the shoppingList variable. The program then prints the entire shopping list to the console. Before reading the file, it's important to check whether it exists using File.Exists. This prevents errors that might occur if the file is not found.

Code Block E.3: Reading Data from a File

```
 1  using System;
 2  using System.IO;
 3
 4  string filePath = "shoppingList.txt";
 5
 6  // Check if the file exists before reading
 7  if (File.Exists(filePath))
 8  {
 9      string shoppingList = File.ReadAllText(filePath);
10      Console.WriteLine("Your Shopping List:");
11      Console.WriteLine(shoppingList);
12  }
13  else
14  {
15      Console.WriteLine("No shopping list found.");
16  }
```

These simple examples demonstrate the basics of using file input and output in C#. Writing to and reading from files can help your program save important data, making it available even after the program has stopped running. By understanding these fundamental concepts, you'll be well-equipped to build applications that persist data effectively.

JSON Serialization and Deserialization

To illustrate how JSON serialization and deserialization can be used, let's consider a simple example of a customer and order hierarchy. Suppose you want to store information about a customer and their orders in a file so that it can be accessed later. Code Block E.4 shows how you could define the Customer and Order classes, and then serialize and deserialize them using JSON.

In this example, we start by defining two classes: Customer and Order (lines 6 through 17). The Customer class has a Name property and a list of Order objects, while the Order class contains details about each order, such as OrderId, ProductName, and Quantity. We then create a Customer object with a couple of orders (lines 20 through 28). We use the JsonSerializer.Serialize method to convert the Customer object into a JSON string (line 32) and save it to a file using File.WriteAllText (line 33). This serialization process allows us to store complex data in a structured, text-based format.

Code Block E.4: JSON Serialization and Deserialization

```
 1  using System;
 2  using System.Collections.Generic;
 3  using System.IO;
 4  using System.Text.Json;
 5
 6  public class Customer
 7  {
 8     public string Name { get; set; }
 9     public List<Order> Orders { get; set; }
10  }
11
12  public class Order
13  {
14     public int OrderId { get; set; }
15     public string ProductName { get; set; }
16     public int Quantity { get; set; }
17  }
18
19  // Create a customer with some orders
20  Customer customer = new Customer
21  {
22     Name = "Alex",
23     Orders = new List<Order>
24     {
25        new Order { OrderId = 1, ProductName = "Laptop", Quantity = 1 },
26        new Order { OrderId = 2, ProductName = "Mouse", Quantity = 2 }
27     }
28  };
29
30  // Serialize the customer to JSON and write to file
31  string filePath = "customerData.json";
32  string jsonString = JsonSerializer.Serialize(customer);
33  File.WriteAllText(filePath, jsonString);
34  Console.WriteLine("Customer data saved to file.");
35
36  // Read the JSON data from file and deserialize it back to a Customer object
37  if (File.Exists(filePath))
38  {
39     string jsonData = File.ReadAllText(filePath);
40     Customer deserializedCustomer = JsonSerializer.
        Deserialize<Customer>(jsonData);
41     Console.WriteLine($"Customer Name: {deserializedCustomer.Name}");
42     foreach (var order in deserializedCustomer.Orders)
43     {
44        Console.Write($"Order ID: {order.OrderId}, ");
45        Console.Write($"Product: {order.ProductName}, ");
46        Console.WriteLine($"Quantity: {order.Quantity}");
47     }
48  }
```

In line 39, we read the JSON data back from the file using
`File.ReadAllText` and convert it back into a `Customer` object using
`JsonSerializer.Deserialize` in line 40. This deserialization process
restores the original object structure, allowing us to work with the data as
if it had never left memory.

Using JSON for serialization and deserialization is particularly
helpful when dealing with complex data structures. It provides a
straightforward way to persist data, making it easy to save and load
structured information whenever needed.

File Input/Output Applied

In this section, we'll explore how Alex could use file input and output
to make his game more flexible and maintainable. One practical way
to do this is by saving crafting recipes to an external file, rather than
hardcoding them directly into the game code. By doing this, Alex can
easily update or add new recipes without needing to recompile the game.
This makes the game easier to expand and reduces the amount of code
that needs to be changed as new items are introduced.

Instead of defining all the recipes in the `CraftingSystem` class, Alex
could create a JSON file called `recipes.json`. This file will store all the
crafting recipes, making it easier to modify or add new ones as needed.
The JSON format allows for structured and readable data storage, which
is perfect for representing complex recipes with multiple components.

Code Block E.5 shows how Alex could implement this functionality in
the `CraftingSystem` class. In this code, the `CraftingSystem` constructor
first checks if the `recipes.json` file exists (line 13). If it does, the recipes
are loaded from the file using `JsonSerializer.Deserialize` (line 17).
If the file does not exist, the `DefineDefaultRecipes` method is called to
create a few default recipes (line 22), which are then serialized to JSON
and saved to the file using `File.WriteAllText` (line 25).

This approach keeps the game flexible and easy to maintain. New
items and crafting recipes can be added by simply editing the JSON file,

without requiring changes to the core game logic. This makes it much easier for Alex to expand the game over time. It also allows for more dynamic game play, as recipes could potentially be updated or modified by players, adding another layer of customization and replayability.

Code Block E.5: Saving Recipes to a File in Alex's Game

```
 1  using System;
 2  using System.Collections.Generic;
 3  using System.IO;
 4  using System.Text.Json;
 5
 6  public class CraftingSystem
 7  {
 8      private List<Recipe> recipes = new List<Recipe>();
 9      private string filePath = "recipes.json";
10
11      public CraftingSystem()
12      {
13          if (File.Exists(filePath))
14          {
15              // Load recipes from the JSON file
16              string jsonString = File.ReadAllText(filePath);
17              recipes = JsonSerializer.Deserialize<List<Recipe>>(jsonString);
18          }
19          else
20          {
21              // Define some default recipes
22              DefineDefaultRecipes();
23              // Save the default recipes to the file
24              string jsonString = JsonSerializer.Serialize(recipes);
25              File.WriteAllText(filePath, jsonString);
26          }
27      }
28
29      private void DefineDefaultRecipes()
30      {
31          recipes.Add(new Recipe("Shield", new ItemType[,]
32          {
33              { ItemType.SolidWood, ItemType.SteelPlate, ItemType.SolidWood },
34              { ItemType.SteelPlate, ItemType.SteelPlate, ItemType.SteelPlate },
35              { ItemType.SolidWood, ItemType.SteelPlate, ItemType.SolidWood }
36          }, new Equipment(ItemType.Shield, 1, 200, 5)));
37
38          recipes.Add(new Recipe("SteelPlate", new ItemType[,]
39          {
40              { ItemType.Steel, ItemType.Steel, ItemType.Steel },
41              { ItemType.Steel, ItemType.Steel, ItemType.Steel },
42              { ItemType.Steel, ItemType.Steel, ItemType.Steel }
43          }, new Resource(ItemType.SteelPlate, 1)));
44
45          recipes.Add(new Recipe("SolidWood", new ItemType[,]
46          {
47              { ItemType.Wood, ItemType.Wood, ItemType.Wood },
48              { ItemType.Wood, ItemType.Wood, ItemType.Wood },
49              { ItemType.Wood, ItemType.Wood, ItemType.Wood }
50          }, new Resource(ItemType.SolidWood, 1)));
51      }
52  }
```

Summary

In this appendix, we explored the use of file input and output as a means to save and retrieve data that persists after our program is finished. We covered the File class and its applicable static methods, which provide straightforward ways to handle reading from and writing to files, making it easier to manage data efficiently.

We also introduced the concept of JSON serialization and deserialization, showing how objects can be stored in a structured, human-readable format that the program can easily read from and write to. Using JSON allows for more complex data representations compared to plain text files, ensuring that the data remain organized and understandable.

We saw how Alex was able to leveraging file storage, serialization, and deserialization for storing crafting recipes. This enabled him to easily expand the game without needing to alter the core code base every time a new recipe is added. This approach simplifies maintaining the game and opens up opportunities for future customization and player-driven content. By applying file input and output in this way, we've seen how essential skills like file management can contribute to building more dynamic and engaging games.

Index